5 HOT PLAYS

Oonagh Duncan – Talk Thirty To Me
Paul Dunn – Offensive Shadows
Daniel Karasik – In Full Light
Hannah Moscovitch – The Russian Play
Michael Rubenfeld – Spain

Edited by Dave Carley

5 Hot Plays

edited by Dave Carley

- **Talk Thirty to Me**
  by Oonagh Duncan
- **Offensive Shadows**
  by Paul Dunn
- **In Full Light**
  by Daniel Karasik
- **The Russian Play**
  by Hannah Moscovitch
- **Spain**
  by Michael Rubenfeld

Playwrights Canada Press
Toronto • Ontario

5 Hot Plays © 2008 Dave Carley
Introduction © 2008 Dave Carley
Talk Thirty to Me © 2007 Oonagh Duncan
Offensive Shadows © 2007 Paul Dunn
In Full Light © 2007 Daniel Karasik
The Russian Play © 2007 Hannah Moscovitch
Spain © 2004 Michael Rubenfeld

The moral rights of the authors are asserted.

Playwrights Canada Press
The Canadian Drama Publisher
215 Spadina Avenue, Suite 230, Toronto, Ontario, CANADA, M5T 2C7
416-703-0013   fax 416-408-3402
orders@playwrightscanada.com • www.playwrightscanada.com

This book would be twice its cover price were it not for the support of Canadian taxpayers through the Government of Canada Book Publishing Industry Development Program, the Canada Council for the Arts, the Ontario Arts Council and the Ontario Media Development Corporation.

  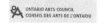 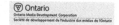

Production Editor: Michael Petrasek
Cover Design: Stéphane Monnet

Library and Archives Canada Cataloguing in Publication

5 hot plays / Dave Carley, editor.

Contents : Talk thirty to me / Oonagh Duncan -- Offensive shadows / Paul Dunn -- In full light / Daniel Karasik -- The Russian play / Hannah Moscovitch -- Spain / Michael Rubenfeld
ISBN 978-0-88754-767-6

1. Canadian drama (English)--21st century. I. Carley, Dave, 1955-
II. Title: Five hot plays.

PS8315.1.F58 2008   C812'.608
C2008-901833-8

First edition: June 2008
Printed and bound by AGMV Marquis at Quebec, Canada

Table of Contents

Introduction

A PLAY IS NOT A PLAY until it has an audience. That might seem self-evident except that it has become common now to regard a two-day workshop as an almost acceptable substitute to production. An immensely-galling-to-writers 'in lieu of.' A number of years ago, George F. Walker referred to the Canadian theatre habit of producing a play once and then tossing it aside forever as 'The Dixie Cup Syndrome.' When he coined that phrase, Walker could never have envisioned the industry that would spring up around new play development. It's a hothouse industry for industry's sake, where theatre professionals gather 'round and create their better Dixie Cup, pat the hopeful playwright gently on the head, then toss. And, as the development industry has grown—and to push the metaphor to its acceptable limits—serial workshopping has become the norm, whereby a play has its initial Dixie Cup moment, is then passed to another theatre where it is worked into a tankard, then gets its handle lopped off before a committee decides it's the wrong colour and style altogether and sends the poor cupmaker packing into the arms of yet another theatre. And so it goes.

Of course there are a few playwrights who can move a play from brain to stage without some heavy lifting from actors, directors and even dramaturges. (Walker is actually one of the few exceptions who springs to mind.) It's just that so many 'works' never exist past the *work*shop. And true, some of the discarded plays are plain bad and keeping them from an audience is an act of artistic mercy. But a discouraging number of theatres use workshops as placebos—in-house exercises designed to wring money from the councils, shore up a weak area of a company's mandate, keep local writers happy, or give actors a grateful bone to chew on while they perform the work of the dead.

When I talk to playwrights and writers' groups I spend a great deal of time wailing about this. I warn them about this giant workshop maw. I urge them to fling themselves and their plays upon the mercy of an audience as quickly as possible. To just go ahead and do it, as the running shoe people so succinctly urge. I give them my very best advice: workshop if necessary but don't necessarily workshop, and hasten yourself to the Fringes.

The five plays in this volume are proof of that sage advice. (I wish I could claim credit for having saved this particular five from terminal workshopping but, by the time I arrived on the scene, they were already thrilling audiences.) I was fresh from having a work of my own produced at the 2007 Toronto Fringe Festival, when the then-publisher of Playwrights Canada Press, Angela Rebeiro, asked me to edit a collection of plays. Because fringing was on our minds, we quickly agreed that a collection of plays that could be produced at small theatre festivals was needed. A collection of potent, portable works that would appeal to a younger demographic. Possibly shorter in length. Exciting and contemporary. Ones that had been produced and would continue to be so.

With those parameters in place, I set out to build this collection. The five plays I've gathered share many qualities but their most important link is their origins in the practical universe of the Fringes. That alone—more than any number of Dixie workshop-Cup warnings from jaded playwrights should make the most compelling case to writers, in addition to being a stand-alone argument in favour of the plays themselves. These five plays grew on their own, sometimes with a little help from established theatres but, most importantly, their authors unflinchingly thrust them before real audiences—and let them become plays.

Where this hot five first appeared is instructive. Four of the plays premiered at Toronto's SummerWorks Festival. Paul Dunn's *Offensive Shadows* and Daniel Karasik's *In Full Light* were produced at the 2007 SummerWorks; Hannah Moscovitch's *The Russian Play* in 2006, and Michael Rubenfeld's *Spain* two summers before that. Oonagh Duncan's *Talk Thirty To Me* premiered at the 2007 Fringe Festival of Toronto.

I have a deep and abiding affection for the Fringe Festival of Toronto— and will wax a bit more on its merits in a moment—but it's not surprising that SummerWorks has yielded such a bounty of good work. SummerWorks has managed to find a formula whereby the ease of production that also allows so many new works to see the light of day at the Fringe (help with box office, publicity and production) is combined with curatorial expertise. SummerWorks was founded in 1991, beginning as an old-fashioned lottery-type festival (albeit one which included a Darwinian crosstown dash to file applications). It became a popular summer try-out spot for plays, but as long as it kept the lottery format, it was seen as a kind of Fringe. However, in 2000 it began to change to a curatorial or juried structure under the leadership of Franco Boni, and became an important factory for new work.

The Fringe still democratically relies primarily on a lottery. (The exception is the Fringe's Bring Your Own Venue applicants, who are vetted by the Fringe staff on different criteria, primarily the excitement factor of their show and the feasibility of their non-traditional performance venue.) The inevitable result of the Fringe's lotto-democracy is, of course, that it features a far higher drek count than does SummerWorks, but this is also curiously part of its appeal. I always work in a day of what I call "pure fringing"—seeing shows of which I have no a priori knowledge, in the hope of stumbling across that rare gem of a script or (more commonly) a great new actor. And, always, there are indeed a handful of plays that become critical and popular hits with the Fringe audience, and which go on to later lives. (The Fringe also has a massive audience; it has become a real people's festival and pulls crowds of people who would never attend regular theatre. SummerWorks appeals more to the 'industry.')

What both festivals offer is an easy and viable forum for new plays and playwrights, to test and showcase their wares in front of real humans. I have no idea if any or all of the five plays in this volume would have received productions if they had had to submit to the conventional workshop/ submit/wait route at mainstream theatres. However, three of them have already had productions post-debut—most notably Michael Rubenfeld's *Spain*, Hannah Moscovitch's *The Russian Play* and Oonagh Duncan's *Talk Thirty To Me*, and I believe all will do so, eventually.

The plays in this volume are also linked in other ways, in addition to their festival birthings. They capture a generation in stasis. They are urban in sensibility. They are eminently stageable. They all seem to feature young people looking for love and (tragically, to my mind) never quite consummating it or, in one or two cases, (less tragically) over-consummating.

There are other, more sinister linkages in this volume. Theatre is an unrepentently incestuous business, and this volume is rife with interpersonal and interprofessional links. I will never forget that wonderful moment in Guillermo Verdecchia and Daniel Brooks's 1991 *The Noam Chomsky Lectures*, when a flow chart of relationships at Theatre Passe Muraille was flashed up on the wall. The line of congruencies and connections and one-degrees of sexual separation had all the appearance of a computer circuit board. *5 Hot Plays* is the same, though (like the plays themselves) generally minus the sex. The writers represented here are not from Toronto, but have all based their careers in that most loathed of all cities. The playwrights are not an ethnically diverse group and, most tellingly in terms of this volume, neither are they demographically diverse. Almost all of them have worked together and, in fact, Michael Rubenfeld has acted in a play of mine and, if that's not incestuous enough, he has recently been appointed Artistic Producer of the same SummerWorks Festival I was just praising. Three of the playwrights— Rubenfeld, Hannah Moscovitch and Paul Dunn—are graduates of the National Theatre School. Moscovitch and Rubenfeld run a small theatre together and Dunn just starred in Moscovitch's Tarragon hit, *East of Berlin*. I could go on.

But I wasn't trying to build a balanced collection; I just wanted to gather five plays that suggested a particular zeitgeist and had qualities of presentation that would allow them to carry on living off the page. Five plays that would collectively crumple the Dixie Cup Syndrome because they are good, fun and whip-smart. But we are Canadian and above all, we prize balance. In future years, we hope to expand upon this volume and bring in work from other communities and regions. But this is the first hot five. The plays in this collection appear alphabetically by author.

OONAGH DUNCAN's play *Talk Thirty to Me* was the first play I selected for this volume and the one that set the thematic light bulb pulsing. The only play of the five with its origins in the Fringe Festival, *Talk Thirty to Me* was the 2007 box office hit of its venue, the Extra Space at Tarragon Theatre. It has since been produced in London, England and New York City, and plans are afoot for a Toronto remount.

The play's appeal to a young theatre audience is obvious—*Talk Thirty* is about them. Over the summer of 2006, Duncan interviewed over fifty Toronto-area twenty-nine-year-olds and asked her subjects how it felt to be teetering on the cusp of thirty (as was Duncan herself). She taped the interviews, and a group of volunteers transcribed them. Duncan calls this method "verbatim" theatre and it shares many similarities with some of the grandest projects in Canadian theatre from—and I note this with a degree of aged horror—some thirty years ago, almost exactly when Duncan's interviewees were gestating. A number of Toronto theatres were producing collective creations back then, Theatre Passe Muraille's *The Farm Show* being perhaps the most famous example.

Duncan's verbatim theatre technique—which she learned at theatre school in England—is a newer take on that process. When she began, the term had just begun appearing in relation to plays such as *Talking to Terrorists* and *The Arab-Israeli Cookbook,* and the only clear definition she got from her teachers was that every word had to have been said by someone in real life—and that it wasn't permissible to "add" things. She could only edit. These strictures separate Duncan's process from plays like *The Laramie Project,* which added material, and those great collective creation plays of the 1970s, which were built on interviews but also included scripted segments and collectively-evolved work.

The eight roles of *Talk Thirty to Me* are meant to be played by four actors—this is a conscious artistic decision and not an economic one. Duncan wanted to have the audience see the actors double, so that they would be reminded to detach words from the image, and see actors as skilled mouthpieces for a number of different interviewees.

The characters of Duncan's play were culled from her fifty interviews and, although they are very distinct, Duncan is quick to point out that she's not attempting to speak for all verging-thirties. She sought out her interviewees from a variety of online sources, and then created composites culled from those interviews. Her subjects were all Torontonians and almost without exception downtown residents. They are highly articulate and depressingly self-absorbed. Twenty-nine does appear to be the new nineteen, if you can believe this play. A professor friend calls Duncan's generation 'snowflakes'—indulgent parents and tiny nuclear families have instilled in them the belief that each one is "unique and special." They aren't, of course, and Duncan's play makes this point. Her twenty-nine-year-olds are united in their self-focus, with the refreshing exception of the one character who has a child. But they are all engaging despite their narcissism, or perhaps because of it, by virtue of their awareness of that narcissism, and their ability to deconstruct their generational concerns.

As mentioned, *Talk Thirty* was an audience favourite and, interestingly, its appeal stretched far past the 556,525 Canadians who were turning 30 in 2007 (Duncan's figures). Older viewers looked back at the angst of a decade-change, with fondness or melancholy, and were reminded forcefully of approaching milestones, usually in multiples of Duncan's focus group. Younger audience members could shiver in anticipation of the horrors that awaited them (though, as I vaguely recall, turning thirty was unimaginable when I had just turned twenty.) The success of the play bears out the strength of Duncan's process; although she is of course pulling authorial strings. *Talk Thirty to Me* has an authenticity that more fictive excursions in theatre often lack. And hence its enduring appeal.

PAUL DUNN's *Offensive Shadows* is the first of four plays given life by Toronto's SummerWorks Festival. Like Duncan's play, it also mines a rich playwriting tradition; in Dunn's case the imaginative extrapolation of characters from Shakespeare. This is a vein that has been tapped with great success in Canadian writing; three examples that quickly spring to mind are Ken Mitchell's *Cruel Tears*, Ann-Marie MacDonald's *Goodnight Desdemona (Good Morning Juliet)* and Djanet Sears's *Harlem Duet*. As with those plays, Dunn has brought a contemporary cast to his play, setting his prequel/sequel to *A Midsummer Night's Dream* in the present, and on the shores of Lake Huron—at the Pinery Provincial Park, to be exact. And, for my heretical money, Dunn has also redeemed the lovers of the Shakespeare play, giving them the spotlight that often eludes them in the original. Hermia, Lysander, Helena and Demetrius are a lot more interesting now that we know their back and after-stories. (To be fair to Mr. Shakespeare, Dunn has had a solid foundation of human folly and love-madness upon which to construct his play.)

Offensive Shadows won the Audience Choice Award at the 2007 Summer-Works Festival and it's not hard to see why: it's funny, tight as a drum and, for any student of Shakespeare, a playful mine of allusions. An important Toronto independent company, Studio 180, gave Dunn material assistance and support for the SummerWorks presentation, and is remounting the play in the Tarragon Extra Space, along with a new short work Dunn is writing about another Shakespeare character, Puck.

Paul Dunn is perhaps the most "experienced" of the playwrights in this volume, having had plays staged over the past decade. Most notably, his *High-Gravel-Blind* was produced at the Stratford Festival in 2002, and had the historic honour of being the first production in that festival's Studio Theatre. Paul is an actor and a graduate of the National Theatre School, an achievement he shares with Michael Rubenfeld (also in the acting program) and Hannah Moscovitch (playwriting). His work as an actor has included stints at Stratford and many of Canada's major regionals and, as mentioned, most recently in Moscovitch's *East of Berlin*. He still regards himself first as an actor, perhaps because he's been doing that longest, but now finds that writing has taken on an equal focus in his life.

Dunn's experience is evident in *Offensive Shadows*, which I would call a traditional well-made play with a clever two-part structure. The first section is the prequel to *A Midsummer Night's Dream* and recounts the hooking-up of the two sets of lovers. Dunn describes it as "*A Midsummer Night's Dream* meets Meatloaf's 'Paradise by the Dashboard Light.'" The prequel foursome are young, horny, and cheerfully—or at least vigorously—dealing with the curve-balls that life throws at them. But when they "wake up" to adult reality—five years and one entire Shakespeare play later—those curveballs are taking their toll. Marriages are foundering, fetishes are flourishing, and the roles they had assumed as highschool students are beginning to look a little, well, highschool. It's time to shake things up. The unresolved yearnings and plot threads of the first section begin to ravel in Dunn's capable hands.

Dunn's characters also are similar to Duncan's, in that they are locked into the same extended adolescence; until the final moments of the play, it is never certain that any of the characters can make an "adult" decision. As Dunn's Hermia says, "We don't want to make choices, or be responsible for them."

Although disguised as a romp, *Offensive Shadows* is a new-fashioned morality tale. Dunn plays his hand in the final moments of the play; things don't work out for the quartet. This is also a theme of this volume—there is an aversion to happy endings that seemingly belie the youth of the playwrights in this volume—aren't the young supposed to be optimistic? It should only be we who have long-passed that thirty-bar who know that everything ends in tears and recrimination. But what does happen in the final moments of *Offensive Shadows* is actually far more interesting than mere tears—Demetrius shows a flash of understanding that promises a happier future, if not for him in his twenties, perhaps when he crosses over into his thirties.

IF I HAD TO PICK ONE WORD to describe Daniel Karasik's *In Full Light*, I'd choose 'haunting.' A teenage girl, Claire, is hit by a car while crossing her street; soon Leon, the car's driver, has insinuated himself into her home and begun appropriating bits of his host family's life. Claire, meanwhile, reaches out to a young birdwatcher across the street, beginning a wary, hopeful *pas de deux* with him even as the situation on her homefront deteriorates. The play is a psychologically intense piece that is full of suggestion and nuance and Leon is one of the most compelling unwanted visitors that I have encountered in theatre.

Karasik began writing *In Full Light* while backpacking in Africa—a world and a half away from the twisting suburbia of his play. He continued developing *In Full Light* with dramaturge Iris Turcott, as part of the Canadian Stage Company's play development program, and he premiered it at the 2007 SummerWorks. As with the other plays in this volume, *In Full Light* is of a length, style and subject matter that makes its production (or at least its 'premiere' production) by a large theatre unlikely.

One of the wonderful things that the smaller festivals promote—because of budgetary constraints, and the need to literally and rapidly clear the decks after each show—is simplicity of staging. Karasik deftly changes scenes by moving heads; a turn or gesture. There is no temptation for set pieces in this play, or in any of the others, because that simply isn't a viable option in a Fringe/SummerWorks setting.

Athough *In Full Light* shares much else with the other plays in this volume, there is one telling difference—it's the only play of the five to feature older characters. This might be a function of Karasik's age—he began writing *In Full Light* when he was nineteen and the play was produced when he was twenty-one. At that age, parents are still an active presence in one's life, and they would be that for the highschool-aged Claire. And Karasik's setting—a suburban street of family homes—is the only one which lends itself to intergenerational contact and conflict.

Karasik allows *In Full Light* to teeter on the edge of plausibility—why on earth would Claire's father Ben ever allow the creepy Leon inside his home?—and this gives the play a seeping aura of tension. Because reality is so skewed, we understand that anything can happen. Leon—mentioned already—is many things, none of them overly salutary. But he can take action, and we never quite know how far he'll go—he's a volatile protagonist and the boarder from hell. Leon's very presence forces the rest of the characters to also act, in relation to him, to each other, and finally upon their unrealized dreams. Whether they can successfully connect is another matter…

The concerns of the two young characters—Claire and birdwatcher Marshall—again echo that of Dunn's *Offensive Shadows* and Duncan's *Talk Thirty To Me*. Claire has been watching Marshall from her window—he, in turn, has been watching the neighbourhood birds, and Claire. When Claire finally begins to reach out to Marshall—once by throwing a rock through his window, but quite possibly also by intentionally running in front of Leon's car—she continues the theme of mis/connecting that runs through all the works in this volume. It is very apparent that, for Claire, at least, it is easier to throw a rock than to kiss. But again—as with Dunn's play—the young, would-be lovers still recognize the importance of trying. At the end of the play, their lips can't quite touch. Dunn—perhaps being a bit older—has allowed his foursome plenty of lip-touching, but ultimately no connecting, even though they concede the importance of making the attempt. Karasik suggests/hopes that more attempts will be made even as that first important reaching-out is not consummated.

HANNAH MOSCOVITCH has burst on to the playwriting scene with seeming effortlessness—she is writing plays for theatres everywhere, and this collection's *The Russian Play* is but one of a number of works currently being produced. Moscovitch has even workshopped some plays but, in her case, they are also getting staged. I once commented to her that her success seemed to be 'overnight' and was met with a horrified denial. The fact is, Moscovitch is twenty-nine (that age!) and has spent ten years slogging through theatre school (she graduated in 2001) and then waitering, all the while writing and laying siege to theatres. In 2002 she founded Absit Omen theatre with Michael Rubenfeld—fulfilling the other half of the breach-the-ramparts strategy (do the Fringes and/or start your own company).

So, although her 'overnight' success is more aptly 'over-decade,' there's no question that *The Russian Play* has been a wonderfully active calling card. Since its premiere at the 2006 SummerWorks Festival, where it won the Jury Prize for Best New Production, it has been remounted at Harbourfront in 2007, and then again in a double bill with Moscovitch's *Essay*, at Factory Theatre in early 2008. *The Russian Play* is shortly to be produced by at least three more theatres, from the east coast to mid-nation, including the Thousand Islands Playhouse in Gananoque, the Chester Playhouse in Nova Scotia, and Winnipeg Jewish Theatre.

Alone of the five playwrights in this volume, Moscovitch has taken her piece into another time and culture. Her central character, Sonya, is a flower shop assistant in Stalin-era Russia who has the misfortune to fall in love with Piotr, a gravedigger. Things between Sonya and Piotr begin promisingly but, as Sonya says, it's a Russian play, with "Some laughing, and then misery!" And when that misery comes, it is unrelenting; Sonya is dumped, fired, thrown on the street, dumped again, imprisoned, and falls ill. Somehow (and this is part of the enduring charm of the play) Sonya manages to retain a rueful sense of humour even as her entire universe conspires to destruct. Her almost casual self-awareness that life isn't a bed of roses for a young flower girl in Russia is in curious contrast with the unrelenting self-awareness of many of the other characters in this volume. But Sonya must understand to survive—or at least to 'bear'—whereas for the young Canadian urbanites who are immersed in self-analysis it is a diversion, a postponement, an evasion.

Moscovitch's characters are (unlike many in the other works in this volume) able to connect but in Piotr's case, he is connecting a bit too frequently and potently. Sonya's life goes to ruin when she rejects the loveless but useful connections of a Stalinist apparatchik, and she is imprisoned. Near the end of her life Piotr the gravedigger does return and, in an act of kindness, gives her some much-needed bread. But even that gift turns toxic for poor

Sonya—once again, a connection has been made and once again it ends in tragedy. .

Moscovitch uses direct audience address; Sonya very clearly tells the audience that this is a play,but such is the poignancy of her story that this bit of deconstruction is never distancing or distracting. Sonya's storytelling charm has thoroughly captured us, and any nod in our direction only underscores the sadness of the story she tells; Sonya's voice is the leavening for the stale bread that is killing her, and breaking our hearts by degrees.

MICHAEL RUBENFELD's *Spain* provokes some pretty intense reactions. I gave a copy to a friend to read and she told me later she questioned my intelligence in including it in a collection designed to showcase hot new work by hot new playwrights. I was surprised, because she normally has excellent taste and I believe *Spain* is an exceptionally strong script. I probed. She resisted. She groused, she denounced. And then I began to understand. I asked her, "Is it the play you hate—or is it Eric and Jared?" Bingo.

Eric and Jared are the two twenty-somethings at the heart of *Spain* and they are probably the epitome of all the indecisive, commitment-averse characters in the five plays of this collection. And Rubenfeld has written them brilliantly; his spare script smacks of reality; it's as close as fiction can ever get to verbatim theatre. They are every woman's nightmare.

When we first meet Jared and Eric, it is right after Eric's girlfriend Beth has returned from a six month stay in Europe. (Eric never did quite learn which country.) In indecently short order, Eric is over at Jared's, chewing over the relationship and it is clear that Eric has been accustomed to talking—apparently ad nauseum—about Beth to his buddy. Jared seems to have spent months listening patiently, though perhaps with reasons of his own. The two young men (one desperately wants to write 'boys') exist in a limbo of inaction: Jared can't finish a documentary (on feces) and Eric has trouble even deciding what kind of tea he will drink. (He's a little more definite about beer.) What they can seem to do is talk about Beth.

Eric really only has one big idea in the play—a disastrous dinner party where he will gather the two main figures in his life and somehow smooth things over. Beth cooks, and the event goes south before the dessert has even appeared. Jared drives the action, revealing that his relationship with Eric is a lot more intimate than Beth can handle. And then, just as it looks like the evening will end in homicide, Rubenfeld drops in a wonderful twist. And he continues to do this throughout the play—subverting our expectations as to what these two monumentally irritating (to my friend) characters will do, with quick plot zigzags.

There are two telling moments near the end of *Spain* which sum up the tone of this volume. Late in the play, despite the disastrous dinner party, Eric and Beth are still living together, still having sex, but not really talking and only seeing each other in the hallway. Passing ships on the way to the washroom. Exasperated, Beth asks Eric what it is that he actually loves about her. Eric—bewildered, as usual, and chronically unwilling to risk an answer, asks her back: "What are you doing?" Exasperated, Beth replies, "Attempting communication." And somewhere, my Jared and Eric-hating friend, out of a bitter well of recognition, is yelling, "It's not worth it, girl!"

Spain ends—as almost all the plays in this collection do—with another attempt at communication, a hug between Jared and Eric. But their relationship has changed. Whatever agenda Jared may have had for Eric has been shelved and, in fact, he has even managed to resume work on his fecal documentary and begun to date a (female) dancer. And Eric is alone, free to terrorize the rest of Canadian womanhood with his indecision.

They hug, but Rubenfeld describes it as a "male" hug, which presumably precludes any possibility of intimacy. They do, in fact, manage to tell each other they love each other, but then they exit to their lives and the viewer gets the impression that something close—if never exactly active—has ended. The importance of communication has again been established and, as with the other plays, the difficulty of connecting has also been carefully laid out. Rubenfeld's ending could be played a variety of ways; it's very open-ended and all the more realistic for being so.

Spain is a tight three-hander, economical in its use of language and setting. As with all of the plays in this volume, it can be produced on and for a dime. It has had two productions—premiering at SummerWorks in 2004 (where it was named Outstanding New Play/Production by *NOW* Magazine), and a remount in October 2006, in the Tarragon Theatre Extra Space. Plans are afoot for more productions.

5 HOT PLAYS from two hot festivals. Inventive, engaging plays that focus on a generation's inability to commit—but written by five writers who have themselves taken the plunge and thrown their plays in front of audiences. In theatre terms, the most admirable commitment of all. And the very act of doing so—and hopefully with the help of their publication in this volume—should ensure some degree of permanence for their (five) (hot) plays.

—Dave Carley, Toronto, 2008

Talk Thirty to Me

a verbatim play by Oonagh Duncan

Oonagh Duncan is a drama graduate of Queens University in Kingston, Ontario, and received her MA in Acting from East 15 Acting School in London, England. While there, she created her first verbatim play, *The Outsider*, as her thesis project. *The Outsider* examines local attitudes about changing demographics in an Essex, England town represented by the anti-immigration British National Party.

Upon returning to Toronto in 2005, Oonagh founded Oyster Productions. The company's mandate is to "tell stories to explore our community and expand our world." Oonagh's second verbatim play was the critically acclaimed Fringe 2007 hit, *Talk Thirty to Me*, which examines the coming of age of twenty-nine-year-olds in an era of extended adolescence. *Talk Thirty to Me* has gained national media attention and has subsequently been presented in London and New York.

Oonagh is currently working on a verbatim follow-up to *Talk Thirty to Me*, about turning sixty. She is also collaborating on a play based on the court transcripts of the 2005 refugee hearing of American war resister and conscientious objector Jeremy Hinzman.

Oonagh Duncan's website is www.oysterproductions.ca

This play is dedicated to Cameron Wright, in recognition of his artistic genius and his awesomeness at thirty.

Production Notes

Talk Thirty to Me was developed from interviews with over fifty Toronto-area twenty-nine-year-olds recorded in the summer of 2006. The playwright interviewed and asked them how they felt about turning thirty. The interviews were transcribed verbatim and edited to create the play text.

This source material was collected during a specific time frame, and in a specific location. As a result, the script contains both topical and local references, and the statistics presented in the slide sections reflect a particular group of twenty-nine-year-olds. Directors of subsequent productions have two choices when approaching the play text. The first is to leave the script intact: a documented archive of a specific group's coming of age. The second is to update and localize the material to suit the production's particular environment. In either case, the glossary below serves as a lexicon for references that may be unfamiliar:

Centennial: A local community college.
The Drake Hotel: A trendy hotel/bar/lounge.
Eaton Centre: A large urban mall in the centre of Toronto.
Flirty Girl Fitness: A gym specializing in pole and lap dance training, etc.
Lavalife: A popular Internet dating service.
NOW Magazine: A local alternative weekly tabloid.
Queen and John: Hip downtown area.
RRSP: A Registered Retirement Savings Plan (similar to a 401K in the US).
Scarborough: A much-maligned suburb (think New Jersey to Manhattan).
Thunder Bay: A small city in the rural north.
"What happened in Montreal the other day": The Dawson College shooting of September 13, 2006.[1]

Talk Thirty to Me includes a multimedia/video component, comprised of a series of slides projected above or behind the performers throughout the play. Screen contents are indicated by the notations "Title Slide" or "Information Slide." Information Slides should have a consistent visual style and support the "documentary" aspects of the play. Most often they comment on dialogue that has just been spoken. Title Slides appear at the beginning of each new section or chapter. They should be visually distinct from the more frequently displayed Information Slides and clearly delineate the different sections of the text.

Acknowledgements

The creation of *Talk Thirty to Me* could have only been possible through the collaboration of many incredible people.

Obviously, the first to be credited are all the twenty-nine-year-olds who took the time to meet me and entrusted me with their stories. I am not mentioning your names for privacy reasons but I am grateful to you all and hope that your thirtieth year was your best one yet.

Also a huge thanks to all the volunteers who painstakingly transcribed the audio testimony—syllable by syllable!—with a special mention for Lina Zambri and Dave Harkness who went above and beyond all expectations in their efforts to get the job done.

Artistically, *Talk Thirty to Me* was greatly aided by:

• The fellow writers who suffered through early versions of the script and gave me advice: Lee MacDougall, Peter Fulton, Yvette Nolan, Shannon Duncan, Matt Murray, Bobby Del Rio, Kiran Friesan, Lisa Codrington

• The brilliant actors who originated and helped develop these roles.

• The vision and energy of director Matt Murray.

• The wonderful Josh Hind.

• And especially dramaturg, Jordan Hall, whose literary and dramatic intelligence is constantly humbling.

A personal thank you to my exceptionally supportive family and friends—especially Shannon, who read every draft, cheered every tiny victory and had rehearsals in her living room for three months.

Talk Thirty to Me was originally produced in July 2007, in the Toronto Fringe Festival, at the Tarragon Theatre Extra Space, with the following company:

MIRA/SAM   Magdalena Alexander
TIM/BEN   Matt Drappel
DAMIEN/JAKE   David Schokking
VANESSA/KENDRA   Rishma Malik

Directed by Matt Murray
Production Design by Josh Hind
Dramaturgy by Jordan Hall

A staged reading of *Talk Thirty to Me* was produced in May 2007 by Oyster Productions, (Oonagh Duncan, Artistic Director), at The Brunswick Theatre, Toronto, with the following company:

MIRA/SAM   Vanessa Burns
TIM/BEN   Spencer Butt
DAMIEN/JAKE   Duane Hall
VANESSA/KENDRA   Heidi Michelle Thomas

Directed by Matt Murray
Production Designed by Josh Hind
Dramaturgy by Jordan Hall

There was a workshop of *Talk Thirty to Me* with the The Bridge Theatre Company (Esther Barlow & Dustin Olson, Artistic Directors), New York City, in December 2007.

Direction and workshop design by Chad M. Brinkman.

Characters

VANESSA, a cosmopolitan workaholic
KENDRA, an earthy lesbian
SAM, a party girl
MIRA, a young mother, recent immigrant from Yugoslavia
DAMIEN, an arrogant, networking actor
JAKE, a pothead philosopher
TIM, a sassy gay boy
BEN, a boy next door

Note: In the premiere performance, four actors played all of these roles, limiting cast size and reinforcing the sense of these characters as amalgams of the original interview subjects.

TALK THIRTY TO ME

As the audience enters, we see an Information Slide: "Inside every thirty-year-old there is an eighteen-year-old wondering 'what happened?'"

The house lights come down. Music plays.[2]

Information Slide: "In 2007, approximately 556,525 Canadians will turn thirty."

Information Slide: "281,225 will be men. 275,300 will be women."[3]

Information Slide: "In the summer of 2006, the playwright interviewed dozens of Toronto-area twenty-nine-year-olds and asked them how they felt about turning thirty."

Information Slide: "This is what they had to say."

Information Slide: "Word for word."

Spotlight up on SAM.

SAM   Are you recording already? Agh! It's all on tape now! Does it have to be about turning thirty?

> *Lights up.*

TIM   It's not something I'm dreading at all!

VANESSA   I think that anybody who's stressing about age is silly—it's the most inevitable thing in the world!

MIRA   Actually, I feel really good about turning thirty.

BEN   I don't feel um… like I'm losing my youth.

DAMIEN   My dad said it was his favourite decade.

KENDRA   It's not something I think about a lot to be honest.

JAKE   I don't have time to dwell on age and status quo.

ALL   I'm a very busy person.

MIRA   I don't think that thirty means it's over—despite what they told us when we were twelve.

JAKE   Yeah, it's so funny… I think as a kid there's the mid-twenties and everything else was just above that.

KENDRA   I always thought I would die at twenty-seven.

SAM   I was supposed to have four children and have long, curly gorgeous hair. I had this image of me wearing short jean shorts and being this… attractive, together, mother.

TIM   I thought that I would know what I was doing. That the experimentation would be over.

JAKE   I thought I'd have the car and no worries about finances, and just do my shit and take trips and enjoy myself and that would be... life.

VANESSA   I thought I'd be married, I thought I'd have my own business. I thought I'd be so set and rolling. Definitely married.

BEN   I didn't think too much about thirty. I guess I thought kids came about that time.

DAMIEN   I have younger cousins who are probably, like, twenty who are all like, 'You're almost thirty! When are you gonna get married? When are you gonna have a baby? You're so old.'

BEN   I just can't—I can't imagine myself saying, 'I'm thirty.' I used to say, 'Oh that guy's thirty, that's so old.' People who are... accomplished, you know? I'm kind of, 'Oh God, I'm thirty now—'

ALL   Did I do everything that I was supposed to?

> *Title Slide: "Like, what the hell did I do with my twenties?"*

> *Information Slide: "Sam: March 18, 1977."*[4]

SAM   I've had, like, quite little direction in my life. Like, when I think about it, university was a bit of a farce, and I didn't work very hard. Like, I was the party girl, everyone thought that was great, and now I look back and I think, 'Oh my God, where did all that come from?' But who knows why we do the things we do at twenty-three and think that they're going to be a good foundation for the rest of our life? I focused a lot on my social life. I think I can say I've passed that grade now. With flying colours and a very special hat. Drinking yourself into oblivion doesn't hold that much of an appeal anymore. If it does, it's a little like that person looks a little out of place. Like, I was at a Wu-Tang concert the other day and I looked around and I was the oldest one there and was like, 'God, can you be thirty at a Wu-Tang concert?' But sometimes I think about parties and things you did when you were a kid.... It's never going to be back again, you know? You know the feeling of getting away with something? Huh. Maybe that's why people have affairs.

> *Information Slide: "Damien: May 1, 1977."*

DAMIEN   Okay. So: I have two thoughts about it, two main thoughts—and then we can spin off into sub-thoughts. The first one is when I was like... twenty-three or something, I made this pact where I have to be movie star by the time I'm thirty and if not, I'm gonna do something else. So now I'm twenty-nine and I'm—you know... I've got a pretty nice profile in the Canadian entertainment industry, but I'm very far from being a movie star. Which, now at the age of twenty-nine, I'm like, 'Oh, I understand why, because it's very, very hard...' But at the time you know the idea of being thirty is like, 'I have to be great,' and now that I'm almost there it's like, 'Shit, I'm supposed to be WHAT? Like, no way buddy, I only have a year.'

On the other hand... I don't want to be a dick about it, but I've done quite a lot. So much so that I'm like, 'What?! I did what?!' Like, I was on the cover of *NOW*, and then I was the subject of this half-hour documentary that followed me around that aired nationally on Bravo. Like, now it's almost stupid for me to come up with things that I want to accomplish.

Information Slide: "Vanessa: June 22, 1977."

VANESSA   I'll turn this off. *(She goes to turn off her cellphone and sees a text message.)* Huh. I've just heard that my friend's mother has died. This is how it is. Electronic communication has changed the way that people interact, in the way that we send off messages and we don't have to deal with the emotional impact. Or with friends: Why bother going out for dinner when we've already caught up over email?

Right. Thirty. Ew! No, seriously, I'm so ready to leave my twenties behind. I mean, I was the youngest consultant in the history of the agency. At the age of twenty-six. Who asks a twenty-six-year-old to consult on their business? Like, come on. I never dated. No boyfriends, no relationships. I bought a house. And then I rolled that over in the Toronto economy and then I bought a bigger house. I was in such a rush! That energy of going like, 'Ah! I don't know what I'm doing next! And who knows! I'll just fly by the seat of my pants!' And suddenly you turn around and it's like, 'I don't want to fly by the seat of my pants. And quite honestly? I don't think it's a good look for me.' I just focused on my career and making more money, and THEN my friends... when I could fit them in. And I stand here and think... did I make the right choice? You know—I should text her... excuse me.

Information Slide: "Ben: July 17, 1976."

BEN   I think I spent a large part of my twenties... doing shit not for me. I was thinking about us; me and my girlfriend. I thought that was important, you know, to be the business guy, and have the title and the card and, kind of... support... us. But, um... we—broke up. Now I'm single for the first time in my life. So I just have to find myself a sugar mama, so I can be on the other side of it. Just kidding. Don't put that in your play.

Yeah, so: I just changed careers, went back to school… got no house, no wife, no kids, no car, and seventy-one cents in my bank account. Not where I thought I'd be at thirty if you asked me when I was twenty.

And I would say that how I feel about that depends on who I'm comparing myself to, to tell you the honest truth. Like my friend Joe—he's kind of the gold standard: He's got, like, a job that he loves doing. He's got the wife, he's got the two kids, he's got his house; you know, it's like the cliché suburban ideal. And, yeah, I want parts of that, yeah for sure… for sure. But then the other half of my friends are either going back to school or doing something they're not too sure about or they don't know quite where they're going and where they fit in and everything like that so it kind of makes it easier, you know? Knowing that I'm not the only player on Team Fuck Up.

Information Slide: "Mira: September 30, 1976."

MIRA   Well, the twenties for me were a wonderful time in many respects but a very difficult time. Like when the baby was first born, every day feels like an agony. The first six months you're just like, 'Oh my God, how am I going to go to sleep, and how will I ever get to have my life back together.' I could only get two hours of sleep at a time and I was very close to seeing visions. We were at Queen and John and we moved all the way to Scarborough, because we needed to be around family—all part of me trying to get over the postpartum depression. And… what I would have to do, if you can imagine, is I would have to rock her, put the stuff into the box—in tears—and as soon as she was wanting to go to sleep, I would put her into the stroller, walk all the way to the Eaton's Centre to get her to go to sleep, and like, stand by the fountain to let her sleep and, meanwhile, rocking back and forth while reading a book. So, I… I can say that I'm pretty *proud* of that. I've accomplished a *lot* for my… in my years. I'm a mom of two-and-a-half-year-old and a step mom to a fourteen-year-old. But, I look at people my age and… most of them are not married. We're the first ones to have kids. I miss just being able to say, 'Oh I'm going to go to a party.' I mean, like, I haven't seen the Drake Hotel. I know that sounds really lame, but I keep on thinking about that. It's like this Shangri-La where all these thirty-somethings are hanging out. And I'm living here in Scarborough with my child, you know, putting her to bed while everyone else is reading beat poetry.

Information Slide: "Jake: November 9, 1976."

JAKE   My values were all screwed up. I worked my ass off. Like, because it's the cultural norm. Get A-pluses at university, and therefore your life will be good and you'll have a good dental plan. Like, lame shit.

Now I realize that we live in this time of privilege where, like, you know, there is a lot of weight and value and this kind of ethos of like being able to go on a personal journey and discover your authentic self, which is new obviously. Like a couple of hundred of years ago you would either become, like, you know—you would do your internship or you would be an indentured servant or whatever. But I do think we live in a privileged time when you can extend your youth to, you know—thirty. But I think once you hit thirty, even with the most generous definition, you fall outside of your youth. So as much as on one hand it feels sort of like I'm anxiety-ridden, I also recognize that I am in a very privileged position to be able to kind a remain youthful in my choices up until thirty. Until now. So that's cool. I guess.

Information Slide: "Kendra: April 6, 1977."

KENDRA   It feels like a big milestone. I always thought I would die at twenty-seven. I don't know why. It was just this thing I had. I never pictured myself older than twenty-seven. So on my twenty-eighth birthday, I was like, 'Wow. Here I am. I didn't really make plans for this. Uh… okay… time to time to figure out what's going on.' So I decided to take the bull by the horns because… I don't have any other youth to spend but the one I've got, so I have to make some decisions and I gotta make them now. So I left my husband… and started dating a woman. That's what happened. I changed my entire life. Now I'm actually in the driver's seat of my own life. I'm sitting here, I'm happy, I've done it. I took this huge risk, huge chance, leaving the person I love dearly, and I'm happy.

It meant starting from scratch now, though. I mean, I was quite— financially, I was set. We were looking for a house and that all suddenly came screeching to a halt. All my friends are having babies and I'm back in a very small apartment. So I'm at this weird strange space where I'm really in control of where my life is going but I had to take a big step back in order to do it.

Information Slide: "Tim: December 21, 1976."

TIM   My brother calls me—the neurosurgeon with the three kids and the fourth on the way. And I love that his life is not my life and no one thinks his life should be mine. There is no direct pressure from my family—nothing like that. But I think anyone is kidding themselves if they don't feel a sense that he's got a real life and I don't. That feeling is there. Anyway, he called to tell me they bought a house in Thunder Bay, which is fantastic. This beautiful forty-acre lot. It's where they want to be. So anyway, he told me that, and… I was… I was really happy for him. But I hung up the phone and I was just like, 'Oh, man.'

And uh… that night I had a *dream*.

I don't remember the circumstances, it was like a family function—but essentially the dream ended… with… my brother repeatedly punching me in the face. `Cause… like… I had pissed him off somehow… with my attitude or whatever. He just started drilling me in the face. And I was going, 'Yeah! Yeah! C'mon—harder, harder! C'mon, snap me out of it.' It was the sense of… the sense of the frustration of, I guess, the people around me, because they see me unhappy. And they want to shake me and shake me out of it. And I go, 'Yeah, I wish I could shake myself out of it, too.' There are times when I wish somebody I love would drill me in the face until I got some sense in me.

Spotlight on Kendra.

KENDRA   Well, it's a very astrologically significant age. It's your Saturn return. It takes the planet Saturn about twenty-nine years to complete its orbit and get back to the same spot it was when you were born. When that happens, it forces you to look at your life and take stock. It can be very painful. That's the way it happened with me—I suddenly got to a point in my life where I realized: I'm an adult now. This isn't "trysies" anymore. This is life and I am not entirely happy and I don't know what it is. It's really distressing.

Title Slide: "The real world."

JAKE   And the way things are in our culture, people say, 'So what do you do?' Meaning: 'What job you do?'

Information Slide: "The average thirty-year-old has had 7.5 jobs in their life."[5]

VANESSA   I think our generation… we were brought up to believe that that we can do anything. It was like—

ALL   'You can be anything you want, you can do anything you want with your life.'

VANESSA   God: 'You could be an astronaut, you could be a ballerina, whatever you want.'

TIM   At twenty, I was like: 'Right on! I'm going to go and do all this stuff!'

SAM   It's like you graduate and you think in five years you are going to be so successful but the reality is that you're just barely getting by.

JAKE   I have a fucking doctorate degree and I'm having a tough time getting a job.

Information Slide: "The average thirty-year-old stands a 35% chance of being unemployed in the next five years."[6]

VANESSA   As soon as I graduated and went into the real world it was as if I was on a treadmill. Or I was one of those little hamsters on a wheel—just keep going, going, going. Like, I would just work. Even if it's totally stupid mindless stuff, as long as my time is spent doing something I always felt as if I would move forward faster and get closer to my destination if I did… more.

TIM   The building I work in looks like a Borg ship and feels like a cave.

VANESSA   I start the day at 7 a.m., I answer an average of three hundred and ten emails a day, I'm at work `til five and then I go to the gym for two hours. When I get home I eat dinner and all I want to do is pass out. I don't want to talk to anyone; I've been talking all day at work. Wow—what a great life I have!

SAM   I'm so sick of waitressing. But it's a means to an end.

TIM   The job I'm in, I wouldn't say it's my career…. It's just kind of… for now. It's… my money-providing job…

JAKE   Which is why I think people panic. They panic when they are turning thirty because they haven't been doing what they should've been doing in the years before.

> *Information Slide: "On average, thirty-year-olds will change their jobs at least twice in the next ten years."[7]*

SAM   I did a string of temp jobs. Which was fine. For a while. It didn't blossom into anything ever. I would work in a place for nine months and at the end my boss would come and say, 'Well, it's time for you to go now, and spread your wings and get a real job now.' And I am looking at her, and it's like a motherly talk and I'm like, 'I don't want a real job. Are you kidding? I'm in this because I want a temp job. I *want* something that is not… committed. Because I'm an artist! Can't you see that? Can't you see that?' And… I started to realize… all I want is a backyard. Oh, I want a backyard! I'll never have a backyard in Toronto at this rate.

> *Information Slide: "The average annual income of Canadians at age thirty: $29,013."[8]*

TIM   Like, how is it that I'm thirty and all I own is, like a laptop and a tent? I don't have a pot to piss in, I don't have an RRSP…. I'm booking an appointment this week to get one, though. Like, let's get serious.

JAKE   The neighbours would come over and I'd be like, 'Hi, I'm Jake. I'm the thirty-year-old son,' and they're like, 'Oh, where do you live?' and I'm like, 'Here.' It's a bit awkward. I remember reading an article about how adolescence, they've now pushed the definition because adolescence was established so long ago—It was fifteen to twenty because that was where you achieved your life skills to go off on your own. And just—the world doesn't work that way anymore. You can't be prepared by twenty.

> *Information Slide: "The average thirty year-old has between $1500 and $19,200 of debt."*[9]

TIM At the end of the day, it's embarrassing to ask your parents for some cash when you are almost thirty years old. I want a real job. Like the kind where they give you dental insurance.

JAKE I don't feel I have any regrets about not having, um, you know, saved money along the way. Like, I really have enjoyed not caring about that and just be willing to live hand-to-mouth and not having an expensive lifestyle. But... I do want to have a proper income while I'm young enough to enjoy it. Like, get four people together and jump out of a helicopter with snowboards on your back, you know? I want to own a nice car and not be the bald guy that's driving around trying to pick up high school girls like a douche bag you know?

> *Information Slide: "If at age twenty you are not a Communist then you have no heart. If at age thirty you are not a Capitalist then you have no brains. (George Bernard Shaw)."*

SAM What I want is a backyard and I'm still living in an apartment. So I went back to school. I was always doing something new, always trying.... I did my publishing certificate at Centennial, started working in the industry and for the first time I had a job that didn't have an ending date. I got signed on and realized that this was it. It's life. I'm working nine-to-five now. I have my job and I have to be there. And I can't be hung over. And I can't be tired. And I can't... wait until five o'clock. So I quit.

TIM I just want to know that I'm using everything I've got. That I'm not letting anything go to waste. Like, my job is just so.... I'm so bored and... it's been five years, it just seems like, that it's *forever*.... I ran into a friend of mine who I went to camp with and she ended up becoming a nurse, specializing in palliative care. And I had her over for dinner, and she said, 'You know, no one on their deathbed is ever saying, "Oh I wish I put more hours in at the office or I wish I made more money..." The people who are really content at the end of their lives did what they wanted to do and followed their passions.' And she talked like this and like, all of these light bulbs started to go off in my head, 'cause everything should be gravy but... it wasn't and I wasn't happy. Now that I'm an adult in the world, what am I here to do?

JAKE I'm moving to Indonesia. Blue sky, sandy beaches, running around with no clothes on, scuba diving... just these things you fantasize about when you're living your normal cubicle life. And one of the reasons I want to go is to challenge cultural norms. Like, why would I get a mortgage and a car and start commuting to the city? Like, this is the next step for me, right? Like, that sounds awful. Not cool whatsoever. And it's depressing for other people to think about. You know, when someone thinks of me I want them to think… well, not that. Not, 'Oh, Jake! He commutes. He has a job and… has a mortgage.' So like I have the opportunity to not do that.

VANESSA   I think that our generation is—everybody is trying to find their "personal vocation" rather than just doing a job and just doing it. And the younger generation—what are they? Generation Y?—Their philosophy is: 'Don't expect me to come to work for you for any extended period of time, I'm gonna come to work for you for six months and then I'm gonna go travelling for three months then I'll go and work somewhere else…' Well, you know what? I kind of like that philosophy. I wish I had travelled more. That's the big one. I said before I turn thirty I was at least going to do a month stint 'round Italy. Yeah, that's not going to happen. I can't take off October—I've got to work. You know: you still have to get that paycheque! I have a house I have to pay for, a car that needs to be paid for—I can't just pack it up and put it in a backpack and leave! Give me a couple more years. I'll probably be doing it around thirty-five… which I feel is kind of pathetic.

TIM   You know how it is… at every age you think, 'I'm old, I'm too old. I can't change now.' You know, I thought that when I was twenty and when you look back you're like, 'Oh my God, I could have done any-thing. I could have done anything, you know… had I just done it.' So I don't wanna act now like it's too late or I can't change.

SAM   I feel like I need a plan. And a really serious plan this time, because I've always had many plans in the past, and I am so good at talking the talk and not walking the walk. But now, at this point in my life I am like, 'What am I waiting for? Oh my God, what am I waiting for, you know?'

VANESSA   I don't know, I mean, I think our generation has a lot going for it, because we've got so many options, but I think we also have the capability to float along and not get anything done. I mean, my dad was given the option to be either a doctor or a lawyer and that was that…

Spotlight on JAKE.

JAKE   I mean you still do meet people who are still in that traditional mould of 'I go to school, I get my education, I go and work, I build my way up through the company, I meet someone nice and we get married and we live in a house and we have children.' You still meet those people. Like, that perception from the fifties where the man comes home from work and the wife comes and makes him a roast and she wears an apron and they have missionary sex or whatever. For me, my wife could come home and be like: "Bitch, clean my shoes!" and I would just go spit, shine, make her some food, and then, you know, we would just get retarded. That's the vision for the new era.

Title Slide: "I don't know if I believe in the dream."

VANESSA   My friend has turned thirty and is getting married. I heard this through an email—we don't make phone calls. When we make huge life decisions you get an email. And I'm just really bummed out about it. Because something changes when they get married. When you turn thirty, you have a lot less friends in your life, I think, you have a lot more acquaintances.

Information Slide: "Of those who will be married, 76% have been married by their early thirties."[10]

TIM   I don't trust it. I don't trust marriage per se. I may be proven differently but, I've just been cheated on a lot.

SAM   My last boyfriend said to me, 'I don't hate you enough to marry you', and we used to laugh about it. He said, 'Do you know of any married couple you would like to be?' And to this day I've never seen one. I can't speak for another generation, but they were sort of, 'Okay, let's get married!' They didn't take into consideration the real importance of it. I think people settled back then.

TIM   And I've tried it. I lived in New York for a year. I was—I fell madly in love with a stupid boy and I moved to New York City. He was in *Hairspray* in New York and um, it was just like his whole world. I was twenty-four and we got an apartment in Manhattan and we got a couch and I was so... ready to settle down. Like I turned into my mother. I did laundry even though there wasn't anything to wash—like I'd get things dirty just to do laundry. It all came crashing down like within, about a month. I stayed for nine—as I say, nine months; just enough to grow a baby full of issues. He was so focused on *Hairspray*. And I finally asked him one day, I said like, 'I have to know: Do you love me or do you love *Hairspray*?' And he said he loved *Hairspray*. I just think that experience made me realize that I will not give one hundred percent of my life over to someone else again. It's quite liberating actually. So I'm the opposite. I'm like, 'I don't want the couch.'

VANESSA I don't know if I believe in the dream. I've just seen too many marriages fail.

> *Information Slide: "16% of those who have married have already divorced by their early thirties."[11]*

SAM I got divorced. And he ended our marriage with a text message. I still have it on my phone. I could show you. It's so stupid. And I thought, 'This is good. I'm free. I'm done.' And I moved into my parents' house the next day. My parents were a little freaked out, but... I didn't feel any sadness. It was just like, I woke up. It was like that. *(snaps fingers)* Instantaneous. It was the perfect break-up. The worst marriage, but the best break up.

TIM I'm not one of those—I'm not anti-marriage. If you want to get married, that's fuckin' awesome, you know. I went to my first gay wedding this summer and that was cool. I will gladly come to your wedding and spend money I don't have on a gift. I will gladly do that but, for myself as far as legally getting married, I will be surprised if that happens.

JAKE I like the idea of getting married. I really do. For one thing, it differentiates that relationship between any other relationship that I've ever had. But more importantly it is actually, like, the party. Celebrating it. With friends and family and everyone we love. And being like, 'This is going to be awesome. I want to celebrate her, I want to celebrate us.' To me, like, you know, it's just the best frick'n bottle of champagne against the bow of the ship ever. My parents have been married for forty years. They still make out in the kitchen. Which is kind of cool and kind of disgusting.

> *Information Slide: "Couples who wait until their mid-thirties to marry are 43% less likely to divorce than those who married earlier."[12]*

> *Spotlight on MIRA.*

MIRA I love everything about being married. When I met my husband. It really wasn't love at first sight. It was love at first sound. I remember hearing his voice and just knowing that was the man. Like... I remember looking for where that voice was coming from because I knew that was the man I was going to marry. And if somebody told me that I would get married that soon, I would be like, 'No, no way. There's no chance for anything like that.' But I just knew, you know? I said, 'My search is over.' I didn't even search at the time but you know? I just thought at the time—and even I think the same thing now... he's the one.

> *Title Slide: "It's a lottery."*

VANESSA   These days, I just want a life partner I can depend on. That's all. It would be nice to live with someone to save money. Like, there's a practical aspect to it. I'm happy for my friends that are involved and getting married, but I do have a little, 'Oh my God how did that work out for you and not for me?'

SAM   Working in the restaurant, you see some couples who seem very happy. And I look at them and I wonder whether it really works.

> *Information Slide: "20% of women and 30% of men are single in their early thirties."[13]*

BEN   I'm finding it weird to be single at this age. Or—I'm just finding it weird to be single. I've never been single before, so.…. But I talked to my friends about shit like that and they're like, 'Yeah… if you do want to be with someone you have to do something about it, you got to put yourself out there.'

VANESSA   People always say that stupid phrase that I wish someone would take out of the human vocabulary: 'You just got to put yourself out there.' Where the fuck is "there"? Is it a ledge or something…?

BEN   Like, I don't know… I should ask people out or talk to the cute girl who looked at me… you know? But that terrifies the shit out of me. I don't think I could do that. I'm hoping it will just work itself out by thirty-five. But that's the thing… that's sort of what I think about… I hope I'm not in the same position five years from now.

VANESSA   I would not be happy waking up at forty-five not in a relationship.

> *Information Slide: "A woman over thirty is more likely to get hit by an A-bomb than find a man. (Fanny Fink in 'Nobody Loves Me.')"*

SAM   My friend who's getting married gave me some advice about the relationship I'm in, she said: 'If you were, you know, forty-five I'd tell you to get over some stuff and just stick with it but you're not, you're young. So get over it, you've got lots of time,' and I was like, 'Okay,' but then I start thinking, what is it? That the older you get, you should… settle?

BEN   Like I never want to say, 'Oh this girl is… oh, you know, nice, funny-smart and I kind of like her and I'm thirty-seven so… fuck it.' I wouldn't want to settle down with someone under those terms you know?

DAMIEN   Settle is not in my vocabulary. That's why I can't find somebody. Because I want it all. I want somebody who's smart. Who's funny. Who's attractive. Who's got a good sense of values. Who's a minx in the sack but not slutty in public. Who's all these things. Who's discovered sushi before. It's a weird thing but at this point in my life, the idea of someone like, 'Sushi, wow. That's so interesting! I've always wanted to try it!' Like, come on. I want you to know sushi and then bring something to me that I've never tried before. Please don't make me help you discover sushi.

VANESSA   The bar is set really high. I just can't... date around right now. It's kinda like... time suckage. I'm a one-date girl. I look at you and I sum you up and I think: 'Are you worth me giving up two hours at the gym or an extra hour of sleep at night?' and usually it's a no so I'm waiting for the one that says, 'Um, yeah. I'm willing to give up an hour of sleep for you.' I haven't had that yet. It would be nice... I'm looking forward to it when it happens.

BEN   Do I have any regrets? No, I don't regret my life with my ex. I wouldn't trade that for like, getting with a bunch of drunken girls at the bar on random nights, you know? Now, could I have used some... more dating experience in those formative years? Yes.

> *Information Slide: "By thirty, 40% of men have had 10 or more sexual partners. So have 15% of women."*[14]

VANESSA   I'm not interested in smokers and I'm not interested in people with baggage. Although maybe it's impossible to find people without baggage at this age. I always say I don't have baggage but I do.

SAM   And, it is like the older you get, the longer you live, the harder it is to meet people, to connect with people. You know? Why is that? You've gained more experience, you have more stuff to share.... Surely everybody else is out there experiencing more or less the same thing...

DAMIEN   I think that in a big city like Toronto, it's very difficult to find a common "soul." It's very difficult, it's a lottery. But at the same time—

ALL   I believe in destiny.

BEN   I never really did a lot of... active... 'I'm going out and looking for someone tonight,' but I'm trying to be a bit more... open to possibilities.... So—

ALL   I'm on Lavalife.

SAM   Just for fun.

BEN · Just to see.

VANESSA   Just for the exploration.

DAMIEN   ˋCause I'm bored.

> *Information Slide: "Twenty million people visit at least one online dating service a month. Their average age: thirty-two."*[15]

VANESSA   I just always... I guess... assumed on some level that eventually with time and patience, you meet the right person. But that's less of an abstract now and more of a, *'fu-uck!'*

SAM   The thing is... I think in terms of relationships at thirty—it's less casual. People might be still having flings and whatever, but there's a much quicker process where you decide whether it's worthwhile and can we envision ourselves being together for awhile? People are obviously less willing to sort of go, 'I don't know, maybe we'll hang out for a year,' and I guess maybe a part of that, for women, is realizing there's a certain window of opportunity here and like, 'I'm not going to fuck around.'

VANESSA   The thing is that the men out there all suck.

SAM   Because the only thing that's real about all this turning thirty bullshit is our eggs are getting old. It's kind of disgusting actually. I'm just picturing these dusty mouldy old eggs that have been sitting there for thirty years.

Spotlight on DAMIEN.

DAMIEN   I'm not worried because I'm not a woman. If I was a woman, I would be very concerned. You see there's a power shift that happens between men and women around the late twenties. Before that it was the guys all wanting to get with the girls and the girls were all like, 'I don't know, what's in it for me?' and now the girls are all like, 'I need to find a father,' and meanwhile the pool of single guys is getting smaller and smaller. Supply and demand. Demand increases and supply decreases. Which increases the value of your average man.

Title Slide: "I have to get my shit together first."

KENDRA   Yup. It's biological. Because statistically if you have children over thirty-five, there's a higher risk of having a difficult pregnancy. Or no pregnancy. And considering your prime childbearing years are like fifteen to thirty-five... I mean, I'm kind of on the far end of that now—not that I'm recommending childbirth at fifteen.

Information Slide: "By age forty, 50% of a woman's eggs are abnormal and the chances of conceiving without a donor egg drop to 7.8%."[16]

BEN   A lot of my friends back home have kids. The difference is that here people are starting to do it on purpose.

JAKE   I do have these sort of weird parental pangs every once in a while, but then I'll just go home and spend three days with my nephews and I'm like: I like when I can give them back.

BEN   I wouldn't say I'm panicking but I thought I would have kids by thirty. I sort of always presumed that would follow along. Now I'm just coming to the realization that that's not... that's not going to happen. I don't want to be *old* for my kids or even for their kids. I want to be a fun grandpa, not the old guy who is just drooling in the corner, you know?

KENDRA   My dad was forty when he had me. Now I realize that he was forty. That's why he didn't have any time or energy for me.

JAKE   On the one hand, I feel like I could do anything at any time in any order. On the other, I just wonder if we're waiting too long... if we are going to be able to have children and then when we do have children, we are going to be older parents... how is that going to affect the next generation?

> *Information Slide: "In 2003, 54% of women giving birth in Ontario were age thirty and older."*[17]

KENDRA   We want to have kids. Ideally she would have one and I would have one and we'd have two and that's that. But... we're lesbians.... It involves some planning. It's not one of those things that might happen and you'll deal with it if it does.

> *Information Slide: "27% of women in their early thirties don't use contraception."*[18]

You have to have an orchestrated effort going on if you're getting a lesbian pregnant. There has to be a turkey baster involved or... something. And that's another thing. We have to get a donor who's willing to give us his sperm without having to be a dad because we don't want that. We want to be the parents. Finding someone like that—you wouldn't believe—guys will toss their sperm away in a condom every night! But as soon as a lesbian asks for it, it's like, 'Oh, no! I want to be a *dad*, I want to be part of the kid's life.' And it's like, 'No, we don't want a dad. We want a little cup. Full. Of your man essence.' And that's it.

BEN   And then, like, I've always said, you know, I'm fine supporting myself. Barely. Were I to get married and have a family, things would have to change. How they would change, I don't know.

KENDRA   I just... have that maternal instinct. Like, I'm always the one holding someone's hair while they're puking.... I mean one of my fears as a woman is—you know... coming to a point in my life and wanting to have children and not being able to.

MIRA   It's so funny, sometimes I hear my girlfriends complaining, 'I can't have a kid, I can't have a kid.' And I'm thinking, 'The time it takes you to think about children, I don't even have that time!' And meanwhile, all these people have disposable cash. I don't even know what that means: disposable cash. Like how does it feel to have cash in your wallet that you can just spend on martinis at the Drake Hotel. I keep thinking of this place. I want to be able to watch my daughter play with a tea set and just be in that moment and not thinking, 'How am I going to get that extra hundred dollars I need for the rent this month?'

KENDRA   A couple of years ago, I was so against kids. I was like, 'I hate kids, I don't want kids.' But I think where I was coming from was that kids represent the fear of 'Omigod, I haven't done everything I wanted to do with my life before I had them.' Because when I think to myself about babies, I think to myself, 'Oh God, I can't do it, for at least another five, six, eight, ten years…' Like, I feel like I have so much to do.

KENDRA, JAKE & BEN   I'd have to get my shit in order first.

MIRA   One of the things when people say… I have to figure things out in order to have a kid…. The thing is, when you have a kid, it makes you figure things out. I remember hearing my dad say, 'No, no, no: You have children first and then you figure out the money.' And I thought, 'Well, Dad, that's the stupidest thing I ever heard in my life.' But it's true. The truth of the matter is that no matter what—even if you are Bill Gates for example, he's probably, like, 'Oh my God how are we going to afford these kids.' No matter how rich you are, it is going to take a huge chunk out of your life.

> *Information Slide: "In 2003, a higher income household could expect to spend $13,820 per child under two years old."*[19]

KENDRA   Yeah, time is a big thing. I don't want to have kids until I have a house and some money, but I don't want to have kids after forty, and that only gives me ten years and whatever happened to Africa? I always wanted to go and volunteer in Africa. When's that going to happen? That's the thing that I resent turning thirty, is that my time is getting… my time on earth is decreasing. That's all.

> *Spotlight on BEN.*

BEN   Yeah, I wouldn't want to be twenty-five years old again but I would like the extra time. Like, time is going so fast! Like, where did the summer go? Look at me—I sound like I'm old. But, um, I think that's one of the things for me about turning thirty that it's entering your adulthood and recognizing the next phase of yourself is entering your old age. Not that being in your thirties is like, grappling with death all the time. But, well, for everyone it sits somewhere in you. I mean that's just being human. You know at some point that you're going to die.

Title Slide: "People die."

DAMIEN   I look in the mirror and I do not—I don't feel like I look any older…

ALL   No, I'm in the best shape of my life!

> *Information Slide: "The average thirty-year-old has lost 10% of their muscle mass."[20]*

TIM   I finally quit smoking.

DAMIEN   I've been going to the gym.

VANESSA   I just went on Weight Watchers.

MIRA   I realized I actually like eating healthy.

TIM   I'm not getting any fatter or hairier.

MIRA   Although…

> *Beat.*

I was looking in a mirror the other day and saw a grey hair and almost lost my mind.

TIM   Yeah… well… I guess… my eyesight at the end of the day a little bit. My eyes are like so strained and tired at the end of the night. I go to bed because my eyes are sore. Like, that's an old person thing!

VANESSA   I notice that I need fucking microdermabrasion like nobody's business. Like my forehead. I definitely can see that I have lines. A few wrinkles can be sexy but not too many. It's like anything: everything in moderation.

DAMIEN   I've got friends that are bald. I find myself checking in the mirror to see if my hair is thinning.

TIM   I've got a bald spot on the top of my head. I know it's there so you don't have to be polite about it. Actually… can you trace it so I can feel if it's gotten any bigger?

> *Information Slide: "25% of men have begun to display baldness by age thirty."[21]*

DAMIEN   I get tired easier. Like my stamina is not—mostly talking from a party point of view—I cannot go out three or four nights in a row. If I go out on one good bender, I'm hungover for two days.

MIRA   The genetic decline is starting; my skin is not as smooth and body parts are slowly sagging. You wake up one morning and your back hurts and you're like, 'Oh my God, it's the beginning of the end!'

VANESSA   Cellulite. I was in yoga the other day doing a twist, happy as can be, dum-de-dum, looking behind me and then all of a sudden I was like, 'What the fuck is that?!'

MIRA   Oh yeah, when you have a baby? It is heartbreaking. Just the sense of ownership over your body. Like… you know… before you have a child it is like, 'Oh, I'm getting a pot belly, I better do some crunches at the gym,' or whatever. It's not like you can say, 'Oh, okay, because of having a child my breasts are now sagging. I'm going to go and—' Do what? Like, what are you going to do? Other than go and get surgery, right?

> *Information Slide: "Women over thirty account for 73% of all cosmetic surgery."*[22]

I mean I have complete compassion for anyone who wants to go to have surgery for getting their boobs done. I've totally considered it—which, okay, for me, it didn't last long because we could never afford it.

VANESSA   Yup. Here it is: *(lifting breasts)* Twenty-five. *(dropping breasts)* Thirty-five.

MIRA   It can make you very sad. Because you just look at them and go, 'Oh my God, those are not mine.' It's hard to get over it, but you do… I mean you see these, like, really old eighty-year-old women going around. And they look so proud but their breasts must be, like, pendulous! You know, like, they must have things, like, hanging off of them! And it's just like they've like accepted it. And that's what I want to do… although… um… I have been going to Flirty Girl Fitness. It's an awesome workout. My arms are like, shaking after the pole dance.

DAMIEN   Okay, things are starting to change. And I never cared—I never cared when I was younger… you know, 'Age happens so big deal!' Now it's like I'm beginning to age, and it's like, 'Oh my God, I'm not supposed to care! I never thought I would care, this is not… part of my values… like, at all.' I think I'm pretty healthy but um…. You know what's weird is I had a friend of mine die. And I hate to even say it out loud—but you know, people die. I know that's not a new revelation. Like, I was thinking about what happened in Montreal the other day and I was like—you know, who wakes up that morning and says like, 'I'm just going to school, that's all I'm doing. I'm not going rock climbing. I'm not skydiving, it's just everyday routine.' That—things like that are hitting a bit closer to home.

> *Information Slide: "The most common ways to die at age thirty:"*
>
> *Information Slide: "Accident (29%)"*

Information Slide: "Suicide (12%)"

Information Slide: "Homicide (10%)"

Information Slide: "Cancer (10%)"

Information Slide: "Heart Disease (7%)"[23]

VANESSA   You think when you're twenty that you're immortal and nothing will happen to the people around you. I started realizing that when you say goodbye to someone it could be....`Cause shit does happen.

MIRA   Yeah, I feel that every time I go back home. I can see the circle of life, you know? I am married, my parents are grandparents and I look at them and think, 'God, they are next.' I try to get back there once every other year. Which means that even if my parents live another twenty years, I will only see them ten more times in my life. And every time I think about that I get really upset.

DAMIEN   It's freaking me out. How quickly my parents are aging, I'm not ready for that.

Spotlight on TIM.

TIM   Earlier this summer I had to go to a wedding and I thought, 'Oh I'm turning thirty,' so I sucked it up and I bought a suit and, like as I was buying the suit I thought, 'Well I'm only going to own one suit, let's face it.' And I remember thinking, 'I should buy a dark one because I'll probably have to wear it to one of my parent's funerals.' Not in a… morbid way. It was just a practical thought that invaded my mind. `Cause like, my dad is seventy. And my mom is sixty-five, I think. They're good—they're healthy, you know. But my mom smokes. She says she doesn't. I mean it's fine but… you know. Anyway, I actually went home after, like the weekend after I bought the suit, just for unrelated—you know just for a visit. And I came back and I put the suit on a couple days later to go to this wedding and uh, I was getting ready and burst into tears. And my roommate's like, 'What's wrong?' And I'm like, 'I just saw my parents and they seem so old and I bought this suit' and I—yeah. I don't know. I felt—I just felt their clock ticking a little bit.

Title Slide: "I don't know where the lines are."

SAM   You know, my mom says repeatedly, 'I don't understand the angst of this younger generation… so angsty. They don't know what they want to do.' Because when you can do anything, when there's nothing holding you back, it becomes a little overwhelming.

JAKE   I think for our generation it's almost like no rules anymore. You can sort of find your own fit and I think we are really lucky that way. My dad is all like, 'By the time I was your age I was running a division of a company.' I'm like: 'Eat it.'

TIM   It is such a privilege, but that privilege and choice becomes crippling. While there's a sense of, 'Oh, I have absolute freedom.' Freedom doesn't come from no boundaries. Freedom comes knowing what the playing field is. And knowing how to play within it. And right now I don't know where I fit. I don't know where the lines are drawn.

KENDRA   Maybe it is a burden but I can't feel sorry for people for having that. I won't be cynical about it. I think it is a really helpful thing to try things out, to have the privilege to say, 'You know I'm going to go down this path for a while,' and then say, 'Ah fuck that, now I'm going to go down this one.' I think ultimately it is very helpful.

Spotlight on SAM.

SAM   But with all this switching around… I feel like I'm late for life… constantly playing catch up. It's a little bit like, 'Jeez, I never thought it would take so long to feel comfortable and satisfied.' On the one hand there's nothing wrong with my life and on the other hand, I'm totally dissatisfied and trying to reconcile that is… frustrating. I mean, it's one thing to be twenty and not know any better… but I totally feel like time's running out. My mum had four kids by the time she was thirty! And I'm like, 'Keep on, have faith that it will pan out eventually,' but there's part of me that thinks that it won't and there's something about that fear, combined with being thirty that's just…. horrible… because I feel like my window is closing…

Information Slide: "If you are thirty, you have about 438,300 hours left in your life."

Information Slide: "Less this one, of course."

Title Slide: "This is all good, trust me"

MIRA   It's funny um… I didn't even know what stress is until I got to Canada, you know? Because everybody has like anxiety, depression and like, I was eleven at the time when the war started in Yugoslavia and at this moment we all thought that nothing could happen to change our ordinary lives. And I mean, it was very developed country— before the war, it was a beautiful country; we had the Alps, we were skiing, everything was so cool—and in one second, everything changed. Like in the worst horror movie. You were actually thinking how to survive, almost on a daily basis. Bullets, shooting snipers…. Can you imagine that? Like thinking, 'Okay, I have to go to the school today and I'm not sure if I'm going to be hit by a sniper.' Just try. I understand you can't because you didn't experience that. I wouldn't probably. I would be like, 'Okay, I tried to understand,' but you can't. You have to experience that, to understand that. I lost a couple of members of my very close family and it has been very hard. So when you think about it—like every problem that we have right now, it's so meaningless. It's nothing compared to that. And it's happening, it's happening even now in some other countries. I always say, 'You know what guys, you just need to spend one month in my past life and you would forget about all the bills, all the depression, all the stress. This is all good, trust me.'

Title Slide: "Who's to say anyone ever does settle?"

Spotlight on VANESSA.

VANESSA   Of course it's cultural. We place value on thirty in this culture. I mean, we all hear, 'Oh, the big Three-O.' So of course that changes our perspective. But still, life's experiences are different for everyone. Should I be "settling down"? I don't know. And who's to say anyone ever does settle? But you have to choose. There's no such thing as life-work balance—it's total bullshit. Life is made up of thousands of decisions everyday and you need to keep yourself in check when you're making these decisions. I kept choosing my career over and over again, I kept choosing going out to the gym rather than out with my friends for drinks and then holy shit seven years have passed. So I would say… look up every once in a while to see where the hell you're going. You know, don't do the gut-check at thirty do it at twenty-one, twenty-two, twenty-three, every birthday, instead of just the end result is thirty. It's not the end at all.

Information Slide: "Both Jesus of Nazareth and the Buddha began their ministries after the age of thirty."[24]

BEN   Yeah, maybe you have to… compromise? But I don't mean settling. Settling to me seems a bit defeatist, whereas compromise has a little bit more of thought put into it.

JAKE   I think with any choice you make there's sort of—you have to deal with a sense of loss, you know? I guess by thirty you've made enough choices to mourn the opposite reality.

Information Slide: "In Jewish Law, a high holiday cantor must be at least thirty. This is because he is humble and broken-hearted, and can thus sincerely pray. (From the Mishna Brura*)"*

TIM   I know… I should just be grateful that I'm thirty and that I'm here. It could be worse. I could have been kidnapped, I could have ended up with one of those guys that that I'm not proud of knowing and ruined my long-term life.

KENDRA   Life is a long period of time. I'm certainly not the same person I was at twenty-two. I bet you're not. And thank goodness I've changed. Thank goodness I've learned a thing or two in eight years.

> *Information Slide: "In his later years Pablo Picasso was not allowed to roam an art gallery unattended, for he had previously been discovered in the act of trying to improve on his old masterpieces."[25]*

SAM   I've learned that I should not drink wearing stilettos.

JAKE   I had a friend who was about to turn thirty and he was kind of wrestling with it so he decided that he needed a coming of age ritual and started doing all this research on the internet about different cultures' kind of initiation ceremonies and designed one for himself where he went into the woods for three days with nothing but an axe. No food. He was like, 'When I came out of there, I was thirty, god-damn it!'

> *Information Slide: "The great thing about getting older is that you don't lose all the other ages you've been. (Madeleine L'Engle)"*

VANESSA   And there's the other side to settling… and that's just being happy with where you are and what you've got. Why is there a negative connotation to that?

SAM   Yeah, I hope I'll think back and think 'Oh, God—I remember when I was so stressed out about turning thirty.' That Saturn thing makes me feel better, though. It makes me feel like Saturn will move on and I'll feel better for it.

> *Information Slide: "On Saturn, a person turning thirty would be one year old."*

DAMIEN   Like, it's just a number. Basically, I'm smarter than I was at twenty and I have a longer resume. I mean, no, maybe I'm not a "movie star." But I'm in a business where, you know, I might hit it huge at fifty, I might hit it huge tomorrow.

> *Information Slide: "At age thirty, Harrison Ford was still four years away from 'Star Wars.'"[26]*

VANESSA   Because I actually feel really young. And, yeah it does feel a little incongruous for thirty. It is also, it's exciting like, 'Oh wow, this is all thirty is?' Apart from the wrinkles which fuck me right off. Un-freakin'-acceptable.

> *Information Slide: "It is good that the young are beautiful; it is the only advantage they have. (William Shakespeare)"*

BEN   I don't know, I just—I wanna be thirty. And be like, 'Wow, I'm not dead yet, there's so much time.' No—I'm excited… is that weird?

MIRA   I feel like all of twenty-nine you're just living in the shadow of thirty and that's kind of lame.

TIM   No one really likes being twenty-nine.

> *Information Slide: "Age is not a particularly interesting subject. Anyone can get old. All you have to do is live long enough. (Don Marquis)"*

SAM   When I turned twenty-six and twenty-seven we had twenty-fifth birthday encores. 'This is my second anniversary of my twenty-fifth birthday,' you know that kind of thing. And then I stopped. Because I'm actually proud of having made it this far. I've made it into adult-hood. And anyway—

ALL   It's not like I'm forty!

SAM   —because I can't even think about that right now. Hey—are you still recording?

> *Blackout.*

Notes

1. Rosie DiManno, "Mayhem and murder on Montreal campus, again," *Toronto Star*. June 14, 2006. http://www.thestar.com/ (accessed May 25, 2007).

2. If rights can be obtained, the playwright's preference is for the song "I'm an Adult Now" by The Pursuit of Happiness. If rights cannot be obtained, an appropriate song in the public domain is recommended.

3. "2006 Canadian Census Data." Statistics Canada. March 13, 2007. http://www12.statcan.ca/english/census/index.cfm (accessed May 27, 2007).

4. As these characters are amalgams of several interview subjects, their fictional birthdays were arbitrarily selected to make them the appropriate age at the time of the premiere performance. Directors who wish to update the text may also wish to update these dates.

5. "Number of Jobs Held, Labour Market Activity, and Earnings Growth Over Two Decades: Results from a Longitudinal Survey." U.S. Department of Labour. Bureau of Labour Statistics. April 2000.

6. *Ibid.*

7. *Ibid.*

8. "2006 Canadian Census Data." Statistics Canada. March 13, 2007. http://www12.statcan.ca/english/census/index.cfm (accessed May 27, 2007).

9. "The Current State of Canadian Family Finances." The Vanier Institute of the Family. January 27, 2005. http://www.vifamily.ca/library/cft/state05.html

10. "Marital and Living Arrangements" U.S. Census. March 1994, quoted in Jonathan Van Gieson et al, *Book of Ages 30* (New York: Crown Publishing Group, 2003).

11. *Ibid.*

12. *Ibid.*

13. *Ibid.*

14. Edward Laumann et al. *The Social Organization of Sexuality: Sexual Practices in the United States.* University of Chicago Press, 2000, quoted in Jonathan Van Gieson et al, *Book of Ages 30* (New York: Crown Publishing Group, 2003).

15.   Gunter J. Hitsch et al. "What Makes You Click: Mate Preferences and Match-ing Outcomes in Online Dating." April 2006. http://home.uchicago.edu/ ~hortacsu/onlinedating.pdf (accessed May 28, 2007).

16.   Page Bierma. "What's Age Got to Do With It?" Consumer Health Inter-active. December 19, 2002. http://www.healthresources.caremark.com/ topic/agefertility (accessed. May 29, 2007).

17.   "2006 Canadian Census Data." Statistics Canada. March 13, 2007. http://www12.statcan.ca/english/census/index.cfm. (accessed May 27, 2007).

18.   Abama et al. "Fertility, Family Planning, and Women's Health: New Data from the 1995 National Survey of Family Growth." CDC/Na-tional Centre for Health Statistics. May 1997, quoted in Jonathan Van Gieson et al, *Book of Ages 30* (New York: Crown Publishing Group, 2003).

19.   Nancy Folbre. "Valuing Parental Time: New Estimates of Expenditures on Children in the United States." January 2, 2002. http://socpol.anu.edu.au/ pdf-files/welfare_folbre.pdf (accessed May 30, 2007).

20.   Edmund Burke. "Will Aging Air Jordan Still Be Able to Fly?" *USA Today*. October 30, 2001, quoted in Jonathan Van Gieson et al, *Book of Ages 30* (New York: Crown Publishing Group, 2003).

21.   "Hair Loss." A.D.A.M. Inc. http://health.yahoo.com, quoted in Jonathan Van Gieson et al, *Book of Ages 30* (New York: Crown Publish-ing Group, 2003).

22.   Jun Ishigooka et al. "Demographic features of patients seeking cos-metic surgery." *Psychiatry and Clinical Neurosciences*. 52 (3), 283–287.

23.   "National Vital Statistics Report." CDC. September 16, 2002, quoted in Jonathan Van Gieson et al, *Book of Ages 30* (New York: Crown Publish-ing Group, 2003).

24.   Jonathan Van Gieson et al. *Book of Ages 30* (New York: Crown Publish-ing Group, 2003).

25.   Unattributed anecdote.

26.   Jonathan Van Gieson et al. *Book of Ages 30* (New York: Crown Publish-ing Group, 2003).

Offensive Shadows

by Paul Dunn

Paul Dunn's play *Offensive Shadows* premiered at the 2007 SummerWorks Theatre Festival, where it won the Audience Choice Award. An earlier drama, 2002's *High-Gravel-Blind*, was the first-ever production in the Stratford Festival's Studio Theatre, and was subsequently recorded for broadcast on CBC Radio. Paul also wrote *Boys*, a one-man show which he performed as part of the Buncha' Young Artists… Festival at Theatre Direct. Paul's plays have been published in the anthologies *Acting Out* and *Gay Monologues and Scenes* (both from Playwrights Canada Press), *Shaking the Stage* (Scirocco), and in *Canadian Theatre Review*.

As an actor, Paul has performed at the Stratford Festival, National Arts Centre, Canadian Stage Company, Tarragon Theatre, Lorraine Kimsa Theatre for Young People, Buddies in Bad Times Theatre, Manitoba Theatre Centre and Citadel Theatre.

A native of Alberta, Paul now lives in Toronto, where he is currently a member of the Tarragon Theatre's Playwrights Unit, and is a guest instructor at the National Theatre School of Canada, from which he graduated in 1998. He is also a graduate of the Theatre Arts Program at Grant MacEwan College in Edmonton, Alberta. Paul is a member of the Playwrights Guild of Canada.

Offensive Shadows was first produced in August 2007 by Athenian Stalls as part of the SummerWorks Festival, at the Tarragon Theatre Extra Space, Toronto, Ontario, with the following company:

DEMETRIUS	Jason Mitchell
HERMIA	Kimwun Perehinec
HELENA	Jessica Greenberg
LYSANDER	Mark McGrinder

Directed by Michael Shamata
Lighting Design by Michael Walton
Stage Managed by Michael Haltrecht
Fight Direction by Joel Harris

Offensive Shadows was developed through the assistance of Studio 180 Theatre in Toronto, Ontario, Canada.

Characters

DEMETRIUS
HERMIA
HELENA
LYSANDER

Notes on Punctuation

/ marks a place where the line following is spoken early, creating overlap.

Acknowledgements

The playwright wishes to thank Michael Shamata for his dramaturgical input, and the following artists for their support in the development of *Offensive Shadows*: Jeff Miller, Joel Greenberg, Rebecca Benson, Andrew Kushnir, Rosemary Rowe and the original cast and crew.

OFFENSIVE SHADOWS

We hear the opening verses of a karaoke version of Meatloaf's "Paradise by the Dashboard Light," performed by HERMIA, HELENA, LYSANDER and DEMETRIUS. They take turns, harmonize (sometimes not so successfully), laugh and whoop it up. The sound of the karaoke brings us into an image of the four lovers in stark lighting, facing the audience. They are in small-town, formal teenage prom wear.

DEMETRIUS   Are you sure that we are awake? It's seems to me that yet we sleep, we dream…

Beat. Nothing. He smacks his forehead a couple of times, as if trying to snap himself out of something. Nothing. He takes a deep breath.

(addressing the audience) We were all very…young. We had been at school together since we were kids—Hermia and Helena. Lysander. And me. And we were still very young when we…

He closes his eyes. Thinks very hard. Then—

It started with a song. I wrote Hermia a song on my guitar, with the two chords I had managed to master. G and D. I was proud of D. D was tricky. Oh, and I had an A-minor, for the bridge. So THREE chords. It worked—

HERMIA   I had to kiss him to shut him up.

DEMETRIUS   Yes. Our first kiss. We dated from Junior High on and I became like a member of the family. Spent weekends practically living at her place, and even went to church with them. Which made her parents real happy. Hermia?

HERMIA shakes her head.

DEMETRIUS   Okay then. *(beat)* Hermia and I had never done it.

HERMIA   Demetrius!

DEMETRIUS   But that was okay by me because I respected her "values." She was my world. My everything. *(beat)* Okay. During the last year of high school, Hermia's family had "adopted" Helena, because Helena's family had moved away to South Africa or Australia or—

HELENA   Zimbabwe, dipshit.

DEMETRIUS   Right.

HELENA   No way was I giving up my senior year for Zimbabwe.

DEMETRIUS   And the two of them were like sisters, sharing a room.

HERMIA   Yes.

HELENA   Totally.

>   *Beat.*

I just loved bunking down with the virgin queen and her Garth Brooks posters—

HERMIA   It was a big sacrifice—

HELENA   Being treated like her charity case, I was very lucky.

HERMIA   But the right thing to do.

HELENA   She was so noble, so noble and so pure. And pretty. Prettiest girl in the whole school, maybe ever. Boys would tell me I'm as pretty as her—

HERMIA   But that was usually when she was going down on them.

HELENA   Which I'm not ashamed of.

HERMIA   Helena used to be taller than me. By like, an inch, if you can believe it—

HELENA   Shut up.

HERMIA   Then I had a massive growth spurt—very late.

HELENA   It was freakish.

HERMIA   Or maybe she shrunk—who knows?

HELENA   WHAT!?

HERMIA   I don't think she's ever gotten over it.

DEMETRIUS   Right. *(beat)* One Friday night I came `round to their house to see Hermia. We had a system where I'd throw rocks up at her window—

HERMIA   He'd seen it in a movie. He never used the doorbell again.

HELENA   Hermia was out, so I opened the window to shout down to Demetrius—

DEMETRIUS   And I hit her in the face with a small rock and she screamed.

HELENA   I had a huge cut, just above my eye.

DEMETRIUS   I begged her to let me in so I could help her clean it up, or take her to the hospital. And she did. And it wasn't that bad—

HELENA   An inch lower and I would've been blinded.

DEMETRIUS   And we were alone in the house. Alone together.

HELENA   And he was swabbing my forehead with cotton balls and peroxide.

DEMETRIUS   And she was crying and I felt so bad.

HELENA   And he was so gentle.

DEMETRIUS   And she was willing. Almost eager.

HELENA   And I was pretty.

DEMETRIUS   She was pretty, too.

HELENA   As pretty as Hermia.

DEMETRIUS   In a different way.

HELENA   Even more so, maybe.

DEMETRIUS   In a... desperate way.

HELENA   I was still a virgin, too. Technically. Down there. *(beat)* We did it on the kitchen floor. It was very hurried and quiet. Only shallow breathing. I didn't even cry out when he pushed into me.

DEMETRIUS   It was a bit awkward. Aren't first times usually?

HELENA   He didn't say anything afterwards except "uh... thanks," and he pulled up his pants and stumbled out the door.

DEMETRIUS   Everything snapped once I'd... I'd...

HELENA   Leaving me on the linoleum with a bleeding forehead and a bleeding—

LYSANDER   Charming. Real smooth, buddy.

DEMETRIUS   I went home and cried.

HELENA   I went up to my room and cried. I missed him so terribly, suddenly.

DEMETRIUS   I tried to write a song.

HELENA   I missed him more than anyone, suddenly. More than my parents.

DEMETRIUS   I tried to make it right in my head.

HELENA   And I waited for him to come back.

> *Beat.*

HERMIA   I'm so glad I waited until marriage.

Beat—HELENA glowers.

LYSANDER That same Friday night, Hermia was at my house.

HERMIA I was his tutor.

LYSANDER Rugby took up a lot of time. I needed a little help and Hermia was in my physics class—

HERMIA Lysander was a songwriter, too.

LYSANDER That's right, buddy.

HERMIA He had more than three chords.

LYSANDER You need more than three, for structure.

HERMIA He had four. And an electric guitar he plugged into an amp.

LYSANDER Rock it out.

HERMIA He wrote powerful heavy metal rock ballads to my eyes. That made me cry they were so beautiful. That Friday night, I had only been tutoring him for half an hour when he said—

LYSANDER "My jock brain is full, Hermia, I need a break, want a soda?"

HERMIA He was always downplaying his smarts. And he plugged in his amp.

LYSANDER "Just a little song I'm working on. About a girl."

HERMIA "Which girl?"

LYSANDER "Guess."

They smile.

HERMIA And then I kissed him.

LYSANDER She kissed me, dude.

DEMETRIUS I know.

HERMIA And I said—"I've got Demetrius." And he said—

LYSANDER "Do you want him?"

HERMIA And I couldn't answer, and so...

LYSANDER I kissed her back.

HERMIA And it was good.

LYSANDER Thanks.

HERMIA And that was that. Settled.

Beat.

HELENA   And so everything was stupid.

    Beat.

HERMIA   The next morning I came downstairs from my room positively floating on air. I could still taste Lysander's full sweet lips from our kiss the night before—

LYSANDER   Yeah, Baby.

HERMIA   I had tingled for the first time. Kissing Lysander had awakened places I thought I had control of, and now they were screaming out— happily. God, you were so hot.

LYSANDER   You too, Babe.

HERMIA   In the kitchen, my father is reading the paper, and my mother is doing the dishes. Without moving his paper away from his face, he says—"Better get pretty. Demetrius is coming over to help me weed." And without thinking I said—"Oh, Daddy, I think I've moved on from Demetrius."

HELENA   I heard the whole thing from upstairs. "No you haven't," he says.

HERMIA   "I've met someone else. Lysander."

HELENA   "That boy we let you tutor? He's trouble—"

HERMIA   "He's very sweet."

HELENA   "Are you trying to embarrass us?"

HERMIA   "No, Daddy."

HELENA   "One boy not good enough for you!?"

HERMIA   "No! I just—please, Daddy—DON'T!"

    HELENA makes a slapping sound, with her hands. Beat.

HELENA   And I'm not going to say what he said next, 'cause it's too awful.

    Beat.

HERMIA   *(softly)* Thanks.

    Beat.

HELENA   But there were tears. And a coffee mug crashing. And Hermia pleading and her father, her father—

HERMIA   He grabbed me by the hair and asked me why I was trying to ruin everything.

HELENA   Lysander was no good. Lysander was the path to immorality.

HERMIA   The path to hell.

LYSANDER   Yeah, Baby.

HERMIA   I was ordered to get upstairs and clean myself up before Demetrius arrived. And to remind myself how lucky I was to have such a good father looking out for me, and such a good man as… as…

DEMETRIUS   As me?

HERMIA   Yes.

HELENA   And I just stayed in bed. Thinking about that good man. Not wanting to wash the smell of him off me.

HERMIA   Um… ewww.

LYSANDER   Teenagers in love.

>   *Beat.*

DEMETRIUS   Okay. So… I got up that morning and decided to propose to Hermia. If I knew that Hermia was mine for real, maybe I could prevent an accident like what happened the night before, with Helena, from ever happening again.

HELENA   Thanks.

DEMETRIUS   It was the only way to make it right. I talked to her dad about it that afternoon. I pulled him aside while we were weeding, and I got his blessing. *(to HERMIA)* I had no idea that he… he…

HERMIA   Doesn't matter.

DEMETRIUS   Right. He even offered to help with the down payment on a ring. Two weeks later, at our high-school graduation, I proposed. It was a big dinner, and Hermia's parents were there, and we were at a table with Helena—

HELENA   The poor orphan.

HERMIA   And Lysander was there too—

DEMETRIUS   At a table of kids too cool to have their parents there. With the rest of the rugby team.

LYSANDER   Having a great time.

HELENA   Demetrius took out the stupid ring and popped the question. Just like that.

HERMIA   In front of everyone.

HELENA   Hermia burst into tears. And her father answered for her.

HERMIA   And I nodded. A reflex of doing what's expected.

DEMETRIUS   Which I took for a yes.

HERMIA   I didn't know what else to do.

DEMETRIUS   And just then, a roar erupted from the rugby table where Lysander had fallen over in his chair.

LYSANDER   I was a little loaded.

DEMETRIUS   Good times.

LYSANDER   Awesome times.

HELENA   Stupid, stupid, times.

> *Beat.*

HERMIA   My father ordered a Scotch for my new fiancé. The son he always wanted.

HELENA   His "main man." He actually said that. It sounded so lame coming from his mouth.

HERMIA   I couldn't breathe, so I excused myself to go to the bathroom. I had mascara running down my face.

HELENA   And I followed. That's what best friends do.

LYSANDER   I was picking myself up off the ground, and my buddies were laughing at me, when I saw Hermia rushing by, covering her face. She looked so unhappy...

DEMETRIUS   "She's just overwhelmed," her mother kept saying. "Because she's so happy. I was the same when Eugene proposed. We were young like you. So young. So in love—"

LYSANDER   So unhappy.

HELENA   Stupid and getting stupider.

LYSANDER   So I get up to follow and crash into Helena. "You all right?"

HELENA   "I'm sorry!"

LYSANDER   "My fault. Is Hermia okay?"

HELENA   Together we follow Hermia to the girls' bathroom. I stand guard as he goes in to talk to her. And I can see Demetrius drinking and toasting with her parents across the room. *(beat)* And I love him.

HERMIA   Lysander didn't say anything to make me feel better. He just kissed me and kissed me with my ugly red tear-stained mascara face. And when I had settled down and could breath again he said—

LYSANDER   "We're getting out of here."

HERMIA   OUT OUT OUT!! He had told me how he would go camping in the summer to this natural park—this campground—where you could walk down through the dunes to the beach at night, in the bright moonlight, you could look up and see every star—

LYSANDER   Look out at the dark water and breathe. And see your future. (*beat*) It was also a great place to bring chicks to get into their pants.

HERMIA   So I said I wanted him to take me there. I needed him to take me there.

LYSANDER   "We'll sneak away. We'll be alone together and figure out what to do."

HERMIA   Maybe we would keep going and never return.

LYSANDER   Maybe we would gather up our courage and go back home.

HERMIA   Or maybe we'd just fuck off and leave them all behind.

> *Beat.*

LYSANDER   Or maybe not.

> *Beat.*

HELENA   An arm reaches out of the bathroom door and pulls me in.

LYSANDER   "Help us!"

HELENA   She was a mess and he was drunk.

DEMETRIUS   Teenagers in love.

HELENA   Both of them, staring at me. Needing me. Suddenly I was the one secret ally to their love. And my mind was racing—does this mean...? If I help them could this mean...?

LYSANDER   Helena was our cover.

HERMIA   Yeah and she was really good at it. How long did it take before she went tattling to her kitchen floor lover?

HELENA   I knew he would want to follow. And I would insist on going to help. Then he would see me for the true heart and devoted girl I was to him. And see who had betrayed him. And be with me again. And be with me forever. I'm not sorry.

DEMETRIUS   And so that night—

HELENA   In the middle of the night—

LYSANDER   I loaded up the truck—a tent, some food, some beer—

HERMIA   And we stole away. Lysander is blaring rock music as we speed along to our destination. He's humming, and I'm staring at the side mirror, watching everything disappear.

DEMETRIUS   Helena tosses rocks up at my window. She tells me the news—

HELENA   "So you see?—"

DEMETRIUS   She keeps saying—

HELENA   "She's gone and I'm here—so you see?" He just stares at me, he doesn't even blink, and says—

DEMETRIUS   "I'll get the car—"

HELENA   And he tosses me a map, and we're off.

DEMETRIUS   In my mom's Chevy—tearing up the highway—

HELENA   In terrible silence. I reach to turn on the radio, or something and—

DEMETRIUS   "Don't touch that!"

HELENA   He slaps my hand away.

DEMETRIUS   "Watch for the turnoff!"—She's acting like this is a road trip!

HELENA   And I stare at the map, then the highway, then the map, thinking—why don't you love me?

HERMIA   We arrive at the campsite and it's just as Lysander described it— the stars, overwhelming—

LYSANDER   I set up the tent and it's time to get cozy—

HERMIA   But I'm tired, so tired and suddenly so alone—with him.

LYSANDER   But she turns away from me and asks—

HERMIA   "One tent? Where's yours?"

LYSANDER   I had only brought one, I thought—

HERMIA   "Well I don't know where you'll be sleeping then."—It comes out of my mouth sounding harsher than I'd like.

LYSANDER   All that open space, and she closes right up.

HELENA   We comb the campground for hours, looking for Lysander's truck. Demetrius keeps pushing me away, but I keep chasing him—

DEMETRIUS   She won't shut up—

HELENA   "Why don't you love me!?"

DEMETRIUS   I can't think, can't see with her clinging to me!

HELENA   He threatens to hit me. Am I really so ugly?

DEMETRIUS   But I don't. I can't. I just leave her instead.

HELENA   And I know then I must be. As ugly as a bear.

LYSANDER   I had managed to stretch out on the picnic table. It was a little hard, and a little cold—but I had smoked a joint and was sleeping pretty good. I wake up to the sound of—

HELENA   "I'm as ugly as a bear!"

LYSANDER   It's Helena, standing over me. The moon is shining through her hair—but where did she come from?

HELENA   He looks at me funny—

LYSANDER   Suddenly so sexy—

HELENA   And I can see in his pants—

LYSANDER   Suddenly so beautiful—

HELENA   Something's not right. He starts whispering "baby baby—"

LYSANDER   Like a change in my vision. Not Hermia, but Helena—

HELENA   I slowly back away.

LYSANDER   I gotta have Helena!

HERMIA   A nightmare. Raccoons sniffing around my head. I wake up screaming for Lysander. But he's gone!

DEMETRIUS   I hear something crying and crashing around in the bushes—

HERMIA   He wouldn't have left me—that would be…. NO!

DEMETRIUS   She runs right into me—my Hermia! She's frantic and fierce—

HERMIA   And completely freaked out now! He won't stop repeating—

DEMETRIUS   "Why don't you love me?—'Cause really, why not?"

HERMIA   I run into the darkness—it's better than him! And where is Lysander?

LYSANDER   Nothing else exists. No one else but—

HELENA   "HELENA BABY, Baby I need you."—Lysander is chasing me. And I'm thinking—

LYSANDER   "Helena, Baby!"

HELENA   Is this some kind of joke?

DEMETRIUS   Outrun and alone—I'm completely alone. I find beer in the back of Lysander's pick-up. It's cheap and warm, but that doesn't stop me—

HERMIA   Where is Lysander?

DEMETRIUS   They still go down easy—

HERMIA   Where the fuck is Lysander!?

DEMETRIUS   Way too easy. I have another and another and /another

HELENA   /I need a place to hide!

DEMETRIUS   and another and—FUCK YOU GUYS!

HELENA   I'm back at the campsite, but I trip over something—a pile of beer bottles and Demetrius on the ground—

DEMETRIUS   It's Helena, suddenly—

HELENA   And he jumps to his feet.

DEMETRIUS   A massive shift, like a blow to the head—I hear Lysander, fucking Lysander say—

LYSANDER   "Out of the way buddy, she's all mine!"

DEMETRIUS   "NO WAY SHE'S MINE!"

HELENA   WHAT?

DEMETRIUS   Did I say that?

HELENA   And suddenly it's—

LYSANDER/DEMETRIUS   "BABY! BABY!!"

HELENA   IN FUCKING STEREO—I get it now. They're making fun of me!

HERMIA   I finally find them and what are they up to!?

HELENA   Poor ugly Helena!

HERMIA   What is she up to!?? I see a bottle on the ground and before I even think—

HELENA   It comes whizzing out of the darkness—just missing my head!

HERMIA   "BITCH!"

HELENA And another and another and her aim really sucks. Then it's—

DEMETRIUS "Control your girlfriend!"

LYSANDER "Fuck you—she's your girlfriend!"

HERMIA "LYSANDER!"

HELENA Oh this just gets funnier and funnier!

HERMIA Lysander won't look at me! He's busy facing off!

LYSANDER Now all I can see is—

DEMETRIUS Him—in the way!

HELENA The boys are taunting, jostling, running—

LYSANDER Down to the beach to settle this like men!

HERMIA Leaving me with a clear path to the man-stealer—

HELENA And me with no choice but to run for my life! Getting lost—

LYSANDER Getting spent—

DEMETRIUS Getting more and more confused—

HERMIA I am fucking amazed. I don't know what to say!

HELENA Had to find a safe place—

HERMIA I just had to lie down—

DEMETRIUS I just had to—

LYSANDER Just had to—

HELENA Just had to—

ALL Sleep.

> *Beat. They recover.*

HERMIA And then the sun came up.

LYSANDER It was the night. The crazy night.

HERMIA We are not those people, we decided. How could we be?

HELENA We came to our senses.

HERMIA Yes. And found our true love, again. Hermia with Lysander—

LYSANDER Of course.

HELENA And Helena with Demetrius. *(to DEMETRIUS)* Told you so. It was the only way. The right way.

DEMETRIUS   Right. That is what happened. Right. But…

> *Beat. DEMETRIUS smacks his forehead a couple of times, again, as if trying to snap himself out of something.*

Are you sure that we are awake?

> *Blackout—more of the karaoke song, giving way to sounds of the wilderness: crickets, waves, and a raccoon screeching.*

> *Night. A campsite. The Pinery Provincial Park in southern Ontario. Two tents. DEMETRIUS is on his knees before the fire pit, where he has assembled a pathetic pile of kindling and some balled up newspaper. He has matches in hand and is attempting to light a fire. HELENA stands behind him, in short shorts and a revealing bikini top, hovering over a camp chair, holding a can of beer and a flashlight. A camp lantern sits on the ground.*

HELENA   You can't even light a fire. What good are you?

DEMETRIUS   *(not looking up)* What's that?

HELENA   Why are you trying to light a fire?

DEMETRIUS   You looked cold.

HELENA   I'm not.

DEMETRIUS   Why don't you put some clothes on?

HELENA   It's warm enough. *(Beat, she drinks.)* Don't you think I look sexy?

> *DEMETRIUS lights a match, tries to light the fire. Blows on it. Nothing.*

HELENA   Demetrius?

DEMETRIUS   Sorry, honey, did you say something?

HELENA   Yeah…

> *She drinks, studies him. He tries another match, fails.*

HELENA   Shoulda brought your Scout manual. *(She cracks herself up.)* You were a Scout right? Your mom showed me pictures. Surely they don't let you be a Scout if you can't light a fucking fire. Hello. *(beat)* Hello? Demetrius!?

DEMETRIUS   What's that about my mother?

HELENA   She's a bitch.

DEMETRIUS   *(looking up)* What?

HELENA   Heard *that*, did you?

DEMETRIUS   Are you being funny again?

HELENA   (*sighing*) Yup.

> *She eyes one of the tents.*

Can you believe those guys?

DEMETRIUS   Huh?

HELENA   It's a beautiful night, we have the whole place to ourselves, we haven't seen each other in years—and the first thing they do is set up their tent and go to sleep!

DEMETRIUS   They're tired.

HELENA   So?

DEMETRIUS   It's a long drive in from the city.

HELENA   So!? We're not OLD people, are we? We should be running WILD ALL NIGHT! (*She shouts to the tent.*) WHOO HOO!

DEMETRIUS   SHHHH!

HELENA   Oh shhh yourself.

DEMETRIUS   When can we tell them?

HELENA   We're not going to.

DEMETRIUS   But I want to.

HELENA   It's too early. It's… bad luck.

> *He lights another match, burns his fingers.*

DEMETRIUS   Ouch. Shoot.

HELENA   Can you believe it's been five years since we were last here?

DEMETRIUS   Um… no.

HELENA   Five years married—do you feel it?

DEMETRIUS   I don't know. I guess. Seems shorter.

HELENA   Seems like ten years.

DEMETRIUS   Okay.

HELENA   Why don't you take your shirt off?

DEMETRIUS   I'm trying to do something here.

HELENA   Used to be you couldn't keep your shirt on. Always walking around, bare-chested. Showing off. When we were here before. Running through the wilderness all tanned and scraped up and… rippling. Like a wild, untamed animal, making me chase you down.

Cut up from the branches of trees, and all sweaty and—come on take it off!

DEMETRIUS   I don't really remember.

HELENA   How could you not? I live for that chase. I wake up still chasing you. Only now you're right there. Right there beside me.

DEMETRIUS   Shoot. I used to be good at fires.

HELENA   Real test of a man's usefulness, this. I ought to be able to trade you in as defective.

HELENA grabs his matches.

DEMETRIUS   Hey!

HELENA   Wake up Lysander. He's good at fires.

DEMETRIUS   Lysander, right.

HELENA   Real useful guy, Lysander.

DEMETRIUS   The wood is damp, y'know, that's why it's so hard.

HELENA   Wet wood. Huh.

DEMETRIUS   Baby please. You're right. He will be able to light the fire. In a jiffy. So I need to get it done first.

HELENA   You men are so sad.

DEMETRIUS   Please. The matches.

HELENA   *(putting the matches down her top, into her cleavage)* Come and get them.

DEMETRIUS doesn't move.

Come on… my rugged man…

He looks away.

DEMETRIUS   Please… *(looks at the tent)* They're right there.

HELENA   Fine. Rub two sticks together—Scout boy. *(She swigs her beer.)*

DEMETRIUS   *(noticing her beer)* What is that?

HELENA   You know what your mother said to me when she was showing me those pictures? She said that she had put you into Scouts to try and settle you down. To try and get you to focus as a kid, because you would never sit still and you were never satisfied unless you were chasing after something. How she would worry and worry about you, because what kind of life would that be? Always chasing and never settling…. She thinks I'm some kind of miracle worker, your mother.

She thinks I managed to get you to focus. (*swigs her beer*) So, is she right?

DEMETRIUS   That's a beer.

HELENA   Uh huh—did I do something to make you boring? Is it my fault?

DEMETRIUS   Honey, you're drinking a beer.

HELENA   Oh, relax. It's one beer. One little camping beer—

DEMETRIUS   The baby, though—

HELENA   What baby?

DEMETRIUS   Helena!

HELENA   Look at me.

> *He looks at her.*

No, at me. Not through me. God, I feel like you never see me. Here. My eyes. What baby?

DEMETRIUS   Honey—

HELENA   You mean the one in here? (*She pats herself, then indicating with thumb and forefinger.*) It's THIS BIG! I've got weeks before anything counts.

DEMETRIUS   Our baby—

HELENA   Our baby wants a beer! Our baby's bored with watching Daddy trying to light a fire and our baby's thirsty—Mama's thirsty!

DEMETRIUS   But honey—

HELENA   Remember Mama? She's right here!

DEMETRIUS   I know—

HELENA   I'm right here!

DEMETRIUS   SHHHH!

HELENA   YOU HAVEN'T TOUCHED ME IN MONTHS!

DEMETRIUS   HELENA!

> *They stare at each other. HELENA drops her empty beer can into the dirt.*

Honey I'm sorry… I'm sorry…

HELENA   Shit.

DEMETRIUS   I'm sorry…

HELENA   Nothing moves you. Nothing.

HERMIA emerges from the tent, fully dressed in clothes way too nice for camping.

HERMIA   I thought you guys had gone to sleep.

HELENA   Why would we? Do we look boring?

HERMIA   Huh?

HELENA   Demetrius is playing caveman. He's trying to light a fire.

HERMIA   Oh—Lysander's good at fires.

DEMETRIUS   We know.

Beat.

HERMIA   Anyway, I'm glad you're up. I... I...

LYSANDER   *(from the tent)* Baby?

HERMIA   Oh god. *(to LYSANDER, in the tent)* I'm going for a pee! *(to HELENA and DEMETRIUS)* Where's the toilet?

DEMETRIUS   *(pointing off)* That way.

LYSANDER   *(poking his head out)* It's far, Baby—just pee in the woods.

HERMIA   I'm not peeing in the fucking woods! I want to pee in a toilet!

She starts off and then stops.

Helena, come with me.

HELENA   Why?

HERMIA   Because it's dark and scary.

LYSANDER   I'll come with you—

HERMIA   NO!

HELENA   Sure. *(looks to DEMETRIUS)* Nothing keeping me here.

She follows, bringing a flashlight. LYSANDER emerges from the tent, shirtless. DEMETRIUS kicks over his assembled pile of kindling, trying to hide the evidence. They look after where the girls have gone. We hear a raccoon chatter, startling HERMIA.

LYSANDER   Huh. I'm just remembering now that Hermia hates camping.

DEMETRIUS   I think she's just remembering that too.

LYSANDER   Yeah...

They chuckle. Stare at each other.

DEMETRIUS   Hope we didn't wake you.

LYSANDER   (*chuckles*) Oh we weren't sleeping.

DEMETRIUS   Oh. Oh, right.

> *Beat.*

Beer?

LYSANDER   Sure.

> *DEMETRIUS gets them beer from the cooler. They drink throughout.*

So—long time no see.

DEMETRIUS   Yup.

LYSANDER   You guys are good?

DEMETRIUS   Oh, yeah, good, sure I mean—normal I guess.

LYSANDER   Happy?

DEMETRIUS   Oh sure. You guys?

LYSANDER   Of course.

> *Beat. They drink.*

DEMETRIUS   (*searching for something to say*) So… how about them Blue Jays?

LYSANDER   What about them?

DEMETRIUS   Um…

LYSANDER   This is the same spot isn't it?

DEMETRIUS   What is?

LYSANDER   As before.

DEMETRIUS   Oh, yeah. Helena picked it out. She insisted it be the same one. Said it was part of the deal.

LYSANDER   What deal?

DEMETRIUS   The pact. The "reunion" pact.

> *LYSANDER laughs.*

LYSANDER   That's right! God, teenagers. We were so… over-the-top. A pact? Who makes a pact?

DEMETRIUS   We're not all that much older now.

LYSANDER   Oh yes we are.

DEMETRIUS swigs his beer.

(spotting something) Huh.

DEMETRIUS   What?

LYSANDER   That picnic table. I wonder if it's the same one. That'd be something, eh?

DEMETRIUS   Yeah.

LYSANDER   And look at that! *(He laughs.)*

DEMETRIUS   What?

LYSANDER   There's the tree we were under when my wife started hurling empty beer bottles at your wife—yelling things I'd never heard come out of her mouth before—

DEMETRIUS   Good thing I brought cans this time.

LYSANDER   *(laughing)* Helena ran away so fast—locked herself in the car. Crazy! Hermia ran off—I think she passed out somewhere in the dunes—

DEMETRIUS   And you and me—

LYSANDER   Racing to the beach, buddy—SHOWDOWN!

He punches DEMETRIUS on the arm. DEMETRIUS flinches.

DEMETRIUS   But we all woke up together. We woke up together back here at the camp and—

LYSANDER   Chalked it up to a crazy dream! The booze, the pot and the stars! Everything was hunky dory! Good times, my friend!

He punches DEMETRIUS on the arm again.

DEMETRIUS   Ow.

LYSANDER   What?

DEMETRIUS rubs his arm, moving away—takes a big swig of beer.

DEMETRIUS   Sometimes I feel like I'm still dreaming. Crazy, eh?

LYSANDER   Good dreams, I hope.

Beat.

DEMETRIUS   Sure. *(beat)* Let's hope tonight will be different.

LYSANDER   I just hope it gets hot. *(He sees the fire pit.)* Were you trying to light a fire?

DEMETRIUS   What?

LYSANDER   Looks like someone made a sad attempt at a fire here.

DEMETRIUS   Wasn't me. I just... you got matches? I ran out.

>   *LYSANDER pulls matches from his pocket.*

Of course you do. The wood is wet.

LYSANDER   Wet wood, huh?

DEMETRIUS   Yeah.

LYSANDER   *(re-arranging kindling)* Let's see what we can do to get that wet wood working...

DEMETRIUS   *(chugging his beer)* Yeah...

LYSANDER   *(lights a match)* Easy baby... *(blowing gently)* there... we... go!

>   *The fire glows. He tosses the matches to DEMETRIUS.*

Here. Take `em—I only need the one. *(He winks.)*

DEMETRIUS   Huh. *(moving to the cooler)* Another beer?

LYSANDER   I'm good. Can't over indulge. I'm on a new workout program. It's kickin'! Check out these abs!

DEMETRIUS   Wow... that's great. Really... *(checking out his own stomach)* ...great.

LYSANDER   *(sucking in to show them off)* Yeah? You like?

DEMETRIUS   Yeah—no—I mean—

LYSANDER   And I can bench two hundred.

DEMETRIUS   I bet.

LYSANDER   You don't sound convinced.

DEMETRIUS   Sure I am—I—

LYSANDER   What, you need proof?

DEMETRIUS   Huh?

LYSANDER   *(cocking his arm for an arm wrestle)* Put her there, buddy!

DEMETRIUS   That's all right.

LYSANDER   What, you chicken? COME ON!

DEMETRIUS   Do we have to?

LYSANDER   `FRAID SO!

LYSANDER gets down on the ground— into arm wrestling position.

YOU GAME, SUCKER!?

DEMETRIUS   Okay, okay. Fine.

He joins LYSANDER on the ground, takes his hand.

LYSANDER   Ready big guy?

DEMETRIUS   "Big guy—?"

LYSANDER   One, two, THREE!

They arm wrestle.

DEMETRIUS   Hah! Looks like somebody's workout program isn't doing it for him!

LYSANDER laughs.

What!?

LYSANDER   Come on, give it all you got!

DEMETRIUS   I am!

LYSANDER   It's your chance to redeem yourself!

DEMETRIUS   What?

LYSANDER   From the ass-kicking I gave you last time!

DEMETRIUS   When!? Down on the beach? You never kicked my ass!

LYSANDER   Kicked it so hard, you still can't sit down!

DEMETRIUS   No! I remember—

LYSANDER   What?

DEMETRIUS   The waves were crashing and the moon—

LYSANDER   The moon was incredibly bright—

DEMETRIUS   And we were cursing and swearing and—

LYSANDER   Naked and sweaty—

DEMETRIUS   And you kept dodging!

LYSANDER   You kept dodging me, chicken!

DEMETRIUS   No!

LYSANDER   Are you giving me anything? 'cause I'm not feeling anything!

DEMETRIUS   You are so full of it! It was over Helena, right?—so I MUST HAVE—

LYSANDER   Over Helena, over Hermia, does it matter? I won! C'mon buddy, try!

DEMETRIUS   You won?

LYSANDER   I got what I wanted. I ended up on top—

LYSANDER swiftly slams DEMETRIUS's hand to the ground.

DEMETRIUS   OW!

LYSANDER   *(laughing)* Sorry dude.

DEMETRIUS   You were holding out on me!

LYSANDER   I didn't want you to feel bad.

DEMETRIUS   Well I do!

LYSANDER   *(laughing)* Sorry.

DEMETRIUS   Christ, what a wimp!

LYSANDER   Don't beat yourself up; you're not strong enough.

DEMETRIUS   Rematch!

LYSANDER   Sorry—them's the breaks!

DEMETRIUS   AGAIN! BEST TWO OUT OF THREE!

LYSANDER   No point! You've let yourself go, my friend.

DEMETRIUS jumps to his feet.

DEMETRIUS   I HAVE NOT!

LYSANDER   Ooo! Oooo! Someone touched a nerve!

DEMETRIUS   I... I...

He calms himself down. LYSANDER just laughs.

No. It's okay. I'm okay.

LYSANDER   Good boy.

DEMETRIUS   You won't tell the girls?

LYSANDER   Oh, now...

DEMETRIUS   Please. I would... I would die.

LYSANDER   I won't.

DEMETRIUS extends his hand to LYSANDER.

DEMETRIUS   Promise?

> *LYSANDER takes his hand.*

LYSANDER   Promise.

DEMETRIUS   Thanks.

LYSANDER   Sure. *(He winks.)* I've missed you, buddy. We don't do this enough.

> *Then, suddenly LYSANDER twists DEMETRIUS's arm, painfully, sending him to the ground—DEMETRIUS cries out.*

YEAH BITCH! TAKE IT LIKE A MAN!

DEMETRIUS   DON'T!

LYSANDER   GOD WHAT A PUSSY YOU ARE!

DEMETRIUS   STOP IT!

> *LYSANDER tosses his hand away and DEMETRIUS collapses to the ground. LYSANDER stands over him.*

LYSANDER   Come on. You love it. You know you do.

> *He leaves. DEMETRIUS is still on the ground.*

DEMETRIUS   *(softly)* Yeah… sure… fine… it's fine… buddy.

> *Blackout. A raccoon screeches. We hear HERMIA in the darkness.*

HERMIA   HELENA! ARE YOU THERE!? Oh God—why are there so many BUGS!? AAHH! AHHHHHH! HELENA!!!!!???

> *HELENA stands on the beach. We hear the waves. The moon is very bright. She searches around with her flashlight.*

HELENA   Hello? HELLO?

> *She stares out at the waves, lost for a moment. A figure creeps up behind her and tackles her. She screams. It is LYSANDER. He is dripping wet and laughing.*

LYSANDER   Gotcha!

HELENA   HOLY SHIT!

LYSANDER   Shouldn't go wandering in the wild at night, all alone—

HELENA   YOU ASSHOLE!

LYSANDER   Someone could do mischief to ya.

HELENA   You're soaking wet! Get off me!

LYSANDER rolls off her and they lie there, looking up at the sky.

LYSANDER   Where's Hermia?

HELENA   I left her in the toilet. She was taking forever. Apparently she can't pee if she's tense, and the woods make her tense.

LYSANDER   Ha.

HELENA   I was standing there, outside the toilet stall, staring down at the beach—she was going on about her new Prada sandals, and how it was a mistake for her to bring them 'cause the wilderness might wreck them, how she should've brought cheap flip-flops like the ones I was wearing—and I thought I saw a beautiful man coming out of the water. His body reflecting the moonlight. Like a vision.

LYSANDER   Yeah?

HELENA   I couldn't help but come down, and look. Turns out it was just you.

LYSANDER   Sorry, I guess.

HELENA   *(still looking up)* Wow. I had forgotten about that.

LYSANDER   What?

HELENA   The stars. Unbelievable.

LYSANDER   I love this beach.

HELENA   Yeah.

LYSANDER   Used to come here and dream all the time.

HELENA   It takes your breath away. Anything could be possible here.

LYSANDER   Yeah. Kinda miss that.

Beat.

HELENA   When I saw that picnic table again, I remembered finding you on it that night—all cold and stoned and…

LYSANDER   And?

HELENA   Horny. Clearly you were very horny—

LYSANDER laughs.

A very horny teenage boy—with chastity girl sleeping by herself in the tent. And out of nowhere you put the moves on me!

LYSANDER   It was a wild night.

Beat. LYSANDER laughs.

She couldn't believe that I hadn't brought two tents—one for each of us.

HELENA   That is so retarded.

LYSANDER   She called me presumptuous and disrespectful.

HELENA   You thought you would sleep in the same tent? Disgusting!

LYSANDER   I know, what a pig. And she wouldn't let me sleep in the truck in case she got attacked by wild animals and I couldn't hear her screams for help. So it was the picnic table or the dirt.

HELENA   Well I hope she's chilled out. You poor guy.

LYSANDER   She's... all right.

HELENA   How are things in the city?

LYSANDER   Busy. Crazy.

HELENA   I envy you.

LYSANDER   I have three offices now. We've expanded.

HELENA   You're such a success.

LYSANDER   I'm barely home. Hermia, on the other hand, is always home. Always home but never free. She's become a socialite—hosting teas and bridge games.

HELENA   Weird.

LYSANDER   Yeah. Sometimes I feel like I'm just her...

HELENA   What?

LYSANDER   Nothing. How's the hometown?

HELENA   The town we never left? Who cares? *(She laughs.)* Most days I feel I'm going to die of boredom. I should've gone to Zimbabwe when I had the chance!

LYSANDER   What, with your folks?

HELENA   Yeah.

LYSANDER   But then you would have missed all of—

HELENA   This. Yeah. *(laughs)* Yeah.

LYSANDER   Right. *(He laughs too. It subsides. Beat. HELENA giggles.)*

HELENA   What if I had said yes?

LYSANDER   That night?

HELENA   Yeah. And we had it off right there on that picnic table.

LYSANDER   Hot.

HELENA   What would've happened?

LYSANDER   Who knows?

> *Beat.*

Do you feel that?

HELENA   What?

LYSANDER   Magic in the air. Something's gonna happen.

> *He giggles. She giggles. It subsides. Beat.*

(*softly*) I need…

HELENA   Shhh. I know. Me too.

> *Beat.*

What were you thinking, putting the moves on me that night?

LYSANDER   You looked so beautiful.

HELENA   `Cause it was dark!

LYSANDER   No. Because you were.

HELENA   As if.

LYSANDER   You are. Like a vision.

HELENA   You weren't making fun of me?

LYSANDER   Poor… sad… low self-esteem… Helena.

> *She kisses him—he pulls away.*

We can find someplace private. Like up against that tree—

HELENA   No.

> *They kiss.*

LYSANDER   Or I could bend you over that rock—

HELENA   OW! NO!

> *They kiss.*

LYSANDER   Okay then—right here.

HELENA   Yes.

> *They kiss.*

Oh God, yes.

LYSANDER   Yeah baby.

> *They continue to make out. Blackout.*

> *A flashlight. DEMETRIUS alone in the woods. HERMIA comes tearing out of the darkness and runs into him.*

HERMIA   OH THANK GOD!

DEMETRIUS   Hermia?

> *She clings to him, sobbing and frantic.*

HERMIA   Your wife left me alone!

DEMETRIUS   What?

HERMIA   I was peeing and she left me, peeing! With no toilet paper!

DEMETRIUS   *(comforting her)* Shhhh…

HERMIA   By MYSELF! And then the door was stuck!

DEMETRIUS   It's okay.

HERMIA   I had to kick it open, and then a raccoon tried to kill me and I got lost. How could she!? She knows I'm directionally challenged!!

DEMETRIUS   Here. Sit down. Catch your breath.

> *She sits, taking his hand.*

HERMIA   I was terrified—no wonder I hate camping.

DEMETRIUS   Camping is stupid.

HERMIA   Self-induced torture. I'm not a fucking hippie.

DEMETRIUS   No, you're a goddess.

HERMIA   What?

DEMETRIUS   What?

> *A beat. They separate their hands.*

HERMIA   You're funny.

> *Beat.*

Does she hate me?

DEMETRIUS   No.

HERMIA   I was trying to be really nice. I was trying to bond, you know? We used to share things—

DEMETRIUS   Sure—

HERMIA   I even said to her—"let's share things!" And she looked at me like I was retarded—

DEMETRIUS   She can be a bit moody—

HERMIA   Is she still weirded out because we used to date? Because you think she'd be over that, I mean—we are—!

DEMETRIUS   Um—

HERMIA   Or is it about money?

DEMETRIUS   What!?

HERMIA   I pointed out my new sandals and she got really offended. I wasn't trying to rub anything in her face! Lysander's been doing so well and I thought she'd be happy for me—!

DEMETRIUS   Oh—

HERMIA   And then she abandons me—what a bitch! How can you take it!?

> *DEMETRIUS is silent.*

Oh my god, I'm sorry.

> *Beat.*

DEMETRIUS   We're doing okay too, you know.

HERMIA   I'm so stupid.

DEMETRIUS   We're… just fine.

HERMIA   I didn't mean that.

DEMETRIUS   And we weren't just dating. We were engaged.

HERMIA   Um… right.

> *Beat.*

DEMETRIUS   We should get you back to that husband of yours.

HERMIA   Oh god no.

DEMETRIUS   What?

HERMIA   I need a break—

DEMETRIUS   Oh.

HERMIA   All I wanted was to go to sleep and he's hot-to-trot.

DEMETRIUS   Really?

HERMIA   There's no stopping him when he's like this.

DEMETRIUS   I take it you're not in the mood?

HERMIA   No!

DEMETRIUS   Gee—why not? He's such a hulk.

HERMIA   *(laughing)* Stop it!

DEMETRIUS   He was showing me those abs of his—very impressive!

HERMIA   HA! Those FUCKING ABS!

> *DEMETRIUS laughs.*

HERMIA   I mean, they're nice and all, but shutup about them already!

DEMETRIUS   Hah!

HERMIA   I don't care about abs, I really don't. He enjoys them more than I do. I think he gets more turned on looking at them than at me—

DEMETRIUS   That can't be true—

HERMIA   Than looking at me naked with my twat in the air!

DEMETRIUS   Um—okay.

HERMIA   I shouldn't be saying such things. I can't help it. You know what he's into now, eh?

DEMETRIUS   What?

HERMIA   Porn. Everything's porn. Everything we do is from some porn. Every position. And the things that come out of his mouth that he expects me to take seriously—while we're doing it—

DEMETRIUS   We don't need to talk about this.

HERMIA   No, it's fine. I'm comfortable around you—

DEMETRIUS   Still, I—

HERMIA   Talking to you has always been like talking to one of my best girlfriends.

DEMETRIUS   Um… thanks.

HERMIA   And I have no one to talk to out there, where we live. And everyone thinks Lysander is just wonderful.

DEMETRIUS   He's a lucky man.

> *Beat.*

HERMIA   You think?

HERMIA stands, brushes herself off—steps forward and looks out.

You can see the beach from here. There's a space in the trees.

DEMETRIUS comes up behind her.

DEMETRIUS   Beautiful.

HERMIA   I can only guess where he has planned—the tent, obviously, or up against a tree... please god, not the beach—I don't wanna be rinsing sand out of my... but yes, that's the porniest isn't it? The beach. That's what he'll want. Oh God! Is there something wrong with me!?

DEMETRIUS   There's nothing wrong with you.

HERMIA   I'm not a prude.

DEMETRIUS   I know.

HERMIA   I'm up for it anytime.

DEMETRIUS   Sure.

HERMIA   Just, with my husband. My husband. Not some porny asshole.

DEMETRIUS   Right.

HERMIA   *(turns to DEMETRIUS)* It makes me so sad. So sad sometimes...

DEMETRIUS   I know.

Beat. HERMIA touches DEMETRIUS's face.

HERMIA   You're so kind and good. I'd forgotten.

Something catches her eye—she breaks from him.

Is that a bush, or a bear?

DEMETRIUS   Where?

HERMIA   Down there, near the water.

DEMETRIUS   *(looking)* Looks like some sort of animal... or two animals, or...

They both recognize it at the same time.

HERMIA/DEMETRIUS   Oh my god.

HERMIA breaks away.

HERMIA   Too dark to tell what it is, really.

DEMETRIUS   *(still staring)* Yup.

HERMIA   So—it's nothing. Nothing at all.

DEMETRIUS   Nope.

HERMIA   Really—nothing...

>   *DEMETRIUS starts to laugh.*

What?

>   *The laughter builds. He sways, off balance.*

You think that's funny?

>   *DEMETRIUS passes out.*

DEMETRIUS!

>   *She retrieves the flashlight and shines it on him, on the ground.*

Oh no... no... no... SHIT! *(She leans down and yells in his ear.)* DEMETRIUS! DEMETRIUS CAN YOU HEAR ME?

>   *A raccoon screeches close by.*

YOU AGAIN!? BACK OFF!

>   *She slaps his cheeks.*

Come on... come on... come back to me!

>   *Huge growl, closer. She screams—*

AHHHHH! GET AWAY!

>   *—and throws the flashlight at it, it goes out. It is pitch black.*

OH THAT WAS DUMB!

>   *Silence. Then—*

DEMETRIUS   Honey?

HERMIA   Oh—thank God! Are you okay?

DEMETRIUS   I was... asleep—

HERMIA   You fainted, are you hurt?

DEMETRIUS   I'm awake now. I... I...

HERMIA   What is it—how do you feel?

DEMETRIUS   I... love you.

HERMIA   Demetrius, it's Hermia.

DEMETRIUS   I know... and.... I love you—

HERMIA   Oh god—did you hit your head?

DEMETRIUS   No—I woke up.

HERMIA   I should check your eyes—let me find that flashlight.

> *She searches around in the dark.*

DEMETRIUS   Honey?

HERMIA   Don't move!

DEMETRIUS   We made a terrible mistake.

HERMIA   What?

DEMETRIUS   You never should have run away from me—

HERMIA   Stop talking—you're in shock.

DEMETRIUS   And I never should have given you up.

> *A match lights in the dark—DEMETRIUS is sitting up, and his face is close to HERMIA's.*

HERMIA   Oh no.

> *HERMIA blows out the match. Blackout.*

> *HELENA, walking really fast, stumbling, with the flashlight—trying to fix her bikini top, which is torn. She is shaken, maybe crying quietly.*

HELENA   *(softly)* I'm sorry… I'm sorry… I'm so sorry…

> *LYSANDER catches up with her.*

LYSANDER   Helena?… Baby?

HELENA   WHAT?

LYSANDER   Baby, I wasn't done—

HELENA   You make a lot of noise.

LYSANDER   Hot, eh?

HELENA   We could've been seen

LYSANDER   You didn't seem to mind.

HELENA   Out in the open like that!

LYSANDER   Made it more exciting, doncha think?

HELENA   It wasn't at all what I expected—

LYSANDER   Huh?

HELENA   I thought I'd feel better—but NO! I FEEL WORSE!

LYSANDER   HEY! It wasn't THAT bad!

HELENA   UGLIER than EVER! UGLY UGLY HELENA!

LYSANDER   BABY!

She stops suddenly and turns on him.

HELENA   *(her top)* This won't stay up, you ripped it.

LYSANDER   Sorry.

HELENA   Why were you so rough?

LYSANDER   Thought you liked it. Didn't you?

HELENA   Banging away at me like I'm some sort of... thing! Some bag of meat! I'm a person, you know!?

LYSANDER   Baby, I—

HELENA   A person with a HUSBAND!

LYSANDER   This bothers you NOW!?

HELENA   Oh God, if he knew he'd be crushed! He would be so hurt, he would cry—

LYSANDER   Pussy.

HELENA   SHUT UP! He's probably still up there, trying to light a fire to keep me warm! Patiently waiting for me! He's sweet and gentle and—

LYSANDER   Hasn't touched you in months.

HELENA   Well no wonder! I don't deserve him! I'm so awful and... restless! I don't deserve him and I don't deserve a... a...

LYSANDER   What?

HELENA   *(an explosion)* WHY DID YOU LET ME DO THAT!?

LYSANDER   We were swept away! It happens!

HELENA   Oh GOD! My poor Demetrius!

She takes off.

LYSANDER   Baby wait—

HELENA   Stop that—I'm not your baby—

LYSANDER   Huh?

HELENA   Hermia's your baby—what's your GODDAMN /PROBLEM!?

LYSANDER   /Oh come on—

HELENA   STAY AWAY FROM ME!!!

She storms off—still holding her top up.

LYSANDER   HELENA!

> *He runs after her.*

> *HERMIA trying to get away from DEMETRIUS.*

DEMETRIUS   I love you!

HERMIA   Will you leave me alone!?

DEMETRIUS   But I love you!

HERMIA   No you don't—you love *Helena,* your *wife,* remember!?

DEMETRIUS   That slut!? Shouldn't surprise me—she was always easy—

HERMIA   She's your wife!

DEMETRIUS   But I love *you!* I always have!

> *HERMIA turns and looks at him.*

HERMIA   You're an idiot.

DEMETRIUS   I'm awake.

HERMIA   You're hurt `cause you caught her—

DEMETRIUS   Yeah—screwing your husband—

HERMIA   But you do love her!

DEMETRIUS   I don't feel it! Not right now! It all feels like a dream—like a spell I was under!

HERMIA   Oh please!

DEMETRIUS   You, on the other hand—

HERMIA   This has nothing to do with me—

DEMETRIUS   You're miserable with a porn addict, a cheater, who—

HERMIA   And you would treat me better?

DEMETRIUS   YES!

HERMIA   This is not an option anymore shithead! And it's none of your business! *(turning out)* A SPELL!!?? What the hell is it about this place!?

DEMETRIUS   I LOVE YOU!

HERMIA   YOU DO NOT!

DEMETRIUS   YES I DO!

HERMIA   WELL—SO WHAT!!???

> *Beat. DEMETRIUS is stunned.*

DEMETRIUS   "So what"?

HERMIA   You know, it's not the woods at all.

DEMETRIUS   What do you mean, "so what"?

HERMIA   It's us. We're assholes. We don't want to make choices, or be responsible for them.

DEMETRIUS   What do you mean—

HERMIA   SHUT UP! GO BACK TO YOUR WIFE! You'd better hope I don't find her first!

> *She takes off. DEMETRIUS stands—stupefied.*

DEMETRIUS   *(softly)* So… what?

> *LYSANDER runs on.*

LYSANDER   Hey buddy.

> *DEMETRIUS stares at him. Beat. LYSANDER laughs.*

Get yourself lost or something?

> *DEMETRIUS takes a deep breath and lets out a mighty roar—he is joined by the roar of raccoons and perhaps a bear. It is loud.*

Holy shit.

> *DEMETRIUS lunges at him. Blackout. A raccoon screeches.*
>
> *HELENA, back at the campsite, sitting, finally managing to fix her bikini top. HERMIA stumbles on. They see each other. Stare. HERMIA is panting, and has lost a sandal.*

HELENA   Hi.

HERMIA   Ripped your top, did you?

HELENA   Yes. It was an accident.

HERMIA   What—a "fucking" accident?

> *Beat.*

HELENA   Oh. Yes. Yes it was.

HERMIA   Well—I'm sure you can get another at the Value Village.

HELENA   Yes. I'm sure I can. Lost a sandal did you?

HERMIA   Yes. One of many things I've lost tonight—

HELENA   Too bad.

HERMIA   Like my sanity.

Beat. They stare at each other.

You know, I've spent way too much time running around scared tonight.

HELENA Yeah?

HERMIA Seeing things I don't want to see and hearing things I don't want to hear.

HELENA Oh yeah?

HERMIA Feeling like if I'm not careful I could get a little wild myself...

HELENA So.

HERMIA So.

> *A beat. Then they lunge at each other and go for the hair. They are locked in a hair pulling match.*

SLUT!

HELENA OH—REAL ORIGINAL!!!... BITCH!

HERMIA OW!

HELENA OW!

> *They stop suddenly, breathless. Then—*

HERMIA `Kay—not the hair.

HELENA `Kay.

> *Beat. Then suddenly HERMIA whips off her remaining sandal and hurls it at HELENA. HELENA ducks.*

HERMIA ARGHHHHH!

HELENA Hey!

HERMIA This is all your fault! This stupid "reunion"! I don't know how I convinced myself it would be a good time! This is the WORST night of my life! I didn't think our last trip to the woods could be surpassed, but I guess I underestimated you!

HELENA You always did!

HERMIA First you abandon me in the toilet—that's like a sacred trust between women and you broke it!

HELENA I couldn't listen to you talk anymore about your awesome life!

HERMIA WHAT!?

HELENA Your life is SO FULL! And you're SO HAPPY!

HERMIA   You think I'm HAPPY!?

HELENA   You've had everything—everything HANDED to you—without even wanting it—or NEEDING it—

HERMIA   I HAVE NOT—YOU SHOULD KNOW!

She lunges at HELENA, who scurries out of the way.

ARRGHHH

HELENA   AHHH!

HERMIA   Damn you and your quick legs! I hope you don't think you're special! You must be number... oh god I've lost count!

HELENA   What?

HERMIA   It's a pastime for him. Like a sport!

HELENA   Oh.

HERMIA   Yeah—you're like soccer to him! Or Ping-Pong! You're not special! You're not pretty! You're just there—

HELENA   Okay.

HERMIA   There, and someone else's—

HELENA   Okay—I get it!

HERMIA   It's just usually a little more DISCREET! So I don't have to SEE IT! So I can choose not to KNOW and... and...

She picks up an empty beer can from the ground, and—

ARGHHHH!

HELENA   DON'T!!

She hurls the empty beer can at HELENA—having no weight, it does not have the desired effect. Beat.

HERMIA   Huh. Bottles are better for that.

HELENA   Yeah.

HERMIA   I can't even hurt you. I want to hurt you so bad!

HELENA   I know.

HERMIA   *(close to tears, an explosion)* You're supposed to be my FRIEND!

HELENA   I know.

HERMIA   OH GOD! Closest thing I have to a friend—you! Isn't that pathetic!?

HELENA Really?

HERMIA REALLY! Lysander keeps saying it takes time—when you move to a city it takes TIME to make… it's been FIVE YEARS and no one… no one shares! So I go on a camping trip with the only people I feel connected to, because they know me, they knew me as I was, when I had a… spirit, but it seems they have all conspired to humiliate me!

HELENA Oh.

HERMIA Fuck you, "Ping-Pong"! You think I have everything!? You want THIS!? You want this so bad!?

HELENA No, of course not—

HERMIA NO! *(breaking down)* OF COURSE NOT!

> *HERMIA gives up and slumps down on the ground—crying.*

HELENA I mean… shit. That is… shitty.

> *Beat. HELENA joins HERMIA on the ground, but still at a distance from her. She continues to cry.*

'Kay—I take it back, you're not happy.

> *HERMIA sobs loudly.*

What are you doing?

HERMIA Shut up—don't look at me!

HELENA Um… okay then.

> *Beat—HERMIA crying.*

Hermia?

HERMIA WHAT!?

HELENA I've got something I want to share.

HERMIA Oh, NOW!? Perfect!

HELENA I'm sorry.

HERMIA WHAT!?

HELENA I really am. I have no interest in Lysander. Besides, it wasn't that good.

> *HERMIA sobs.*

Something snapped in me when I… this was not about you! This was not to hurt you so stop… just stop crying I feel awful.

HERMIA I should think so!

HELENA   I want this all to go away. Pretend it was just a dream—

HERMIA   HA!

HELENA   A nightmare. I've been horrible. Demetrius, he... he loves me, you know? He actually loves me.

> *HERMIA looks up.*

HERMIA   You sure about that?

HELENA   I am. And I think I'm ready to... to try harder, you know, with him. For him.

HERMIA   Good for you. Good luck with that.

HELENA   I'm sorry, Hermia. I'm sorry for... everything.

HERMIA   Oh. Um... okay then.

HELENA   Good. *(beat)* Sisters?

HERMIA   *(laughs quietly—at a loss)* Sisters, sisters... sure.

HELENA   And another thing I want to share—

HERMIA   What—more?

HELENA   Yes. You deserve more of a friend. You do.

HERMIA   I know.

HELENA   And I could... I could use one too.

HERMIA   Oh?

HELENA   Yes, I'm... we're all alone too, y'know, we... I don't have many... I'm...

HERMIA   What!?

HELENA   I'm pregnant.

> *Beat.*

Isn't that... something? I haven't told anyone yet. So there, see?—I'm reaching out... *(smiling)* You're the first. I don't think I wanted it to be true, but now I—

HERMIA   *(getting up and regarding HELENA)* You? You're pregnant?

HELENA   Yes.

> *Beat.*

HERMIA   *(softly, a realization)* I... I... hate you.

Enter DEMETRIUS and LYSANDER—locked in a wrestling hold. Unaware of the girls.

LYSANDER   You've got more fight in you this time!

DEMETRIUS   ARGHHH!

LYSANDER   I like it!

DEMETRIUS   ARGHHH!

LYSANDER   Too bad it's not enough!

He brings DEMETRIUS to the ground.

DEMETRIUS   NO!

LYSANDER   `FRAID SO!

DEMETRIUS   *(still struggling)* WHY CAN'T I EVER WIN!?

LYSANDER   Because that's my job! C'mon, buddy—FIGHT!

DEMETRIUS   DAMMIT!

He pins him to the ground.

LYSANDER   There you go, buddy. On top. Just like last time.

DEMETRIUS   *(struggles)* FUCK!

LYSANDER   BEATEN AGAIN!

HERMIA   LYSANDER STOP IT!!

DEMETRIUS   I... I...

LYSANDER   YEAH?'

DEMETRIUS   I WANT OUT!

LYSANDER   HUH?

DEMETRIUS   I WANT OUT—AND I GIVE UP!

LYSANDER   WHAT?

DEMETRIUS   I GIVE UP /I GIVE UP—

HERMIA   /LYSANDER LET HIM GO!

DEMETRIUS   I GIVE UP!

DEMETRIUS stops struggling suddenly and lies, panting. LYSANDER doesn't know what to do.

LYSANDER   Well it's no fun if you're just gonna—

DEMETRIUS *(breathless)* You will always win… okay? You will always win, always… conquer and you will get whatever you want for the rest of your life… and no one will ever stop you and if they try they will fail and… the only choice they will have is to convince themselves that they're okay being beaten…that they like their place… on the bottom—

LYSANDER What are you talking about—?

DEMETRIUS You won!…. Five years ago you won… she chose you over me and I thought… I could be miserable losing or I could choose to make it okay, take the consolation prize… the leftover… and want THAT!

HELENA Oh god—

LYSANDER Buddy—

DEMETRIUS Pretend I never wanted to win in the first place… pretend I never wanted WHAT I WANTED!

HELENA Oh god—

LYSANDER Dude you gotta stop talking now!

DEMETRIUS I never knew what that feeling was—that fog in my head, like I've been dreaming all this time! You have my wife, you have my past, my hope, the future I wish I had—

LYSANDER I thought we were just playing, dude.

DEMETRIUS All those wasted years! I'm… so… angry! But there's nothing I can do about it, I can't beat you. I can't get them back. I give up. You win.

LYSANDER Oh. *(beat)* Okay then.

> *An owl hoots. Beat. HERMIA steps forward.*

HERMIA Humiliation abounds tonight, I see. *(beat)* Lysander?

LYSANDER Baby… where've you been?

HERMIA Does it matter? I know where you've been.

> *Beat. He looks to HELENA, who looks away.*

LYSANDER Baby, I… don't know what to say…

HERMIA Take me home.

LYSANDER Baby?

HERMIA Now.

He moves toward the tent.

Forget the tent.

LYSANDER   But—

HERMIA   We're never camping again.

LYSANDER   I'll… I'll start the car.

HERMIA   And for Christ sake put a shirt on.

He leaves. HERMIA turns to HELENA.

(to HELENA) Sister.

HELENA   Yeah?

HERMIA   I pictured the two of us having tea on our back porch—we've had a beautiful new rose garden just put in—and reminiscing about different boys in high school, you know?

HELENA   That sounds nice. But…

HERMIA   Yeah.

She goes to leave and stops over DEMETRIUS, still on the ground. Looks at him but says nothing. She leaves. HELENA and DEMETRIUS alone.

HELENA   Demetrius?

He sits up, facing away.

Look at me?

He turns slowly to look at her.

Oh God.

DEMETRIUS   What?

HELENA   You finally see me.

DEMETRIUS   Yes.

HELENA   What do you see?

DEMETRIUS   You're Helena.

HELENA   Yes?

DEMETRIUS   Just Helena.

HELENA   "Consolation prize"?

Silence.

HELENA   Is it… irreversible?

DEMETRIUS   I woke up.

HELENA   It's crazy out here. Things happen. People get… swept away.

DEMETRIUS   We make things happen. We want things to happen. You must have wanted me to see—

HELENA   I don't know

DEMETRIUS   To move me.

HELENA   I'm so sorry.

DEMETRIUS   I'm not.

>   *Beat.*

HELENA   I love you. I'd forgotten that. Can you understand that?

>   *DEMETRIUS is silent.*

We can work it out… We'll be honest with each other and… communicate, and stuff, right? We'll watch Oprah every day and do whatever she says—

>   *DEMETRIUS is silent.*

We could have a family soon. I think I might be ready to… settle. *(beat)* Demetrius, say something.

>   *Beat.*

DEMETRIUS   I'm not sure I ever loved you.

>   *Two beats.*

HELENA   Oh.

>   *Beat.*

DEMETRIUS   But at least I… we… tried.

>   *Blackout.*

>   *The end.*

In Full Light

by Daniel Karasik

Daniel Karasik wrote *In Full Light* in 2006, when he was nineteen years old and backpacking in West Africa. The play was developed the following year at the Canadian Stage Company in Toronto and it premiered at the 2007 SummerWorks Theatre Festival, where it won the Contra Guys Award for Outstanding New Play.

Daniel's other theatre writing credits include *Dances Through Disaster* (SummerWorks 2005), *Night's Swift Dragons* (Rhubarb! Festival 2004), *Port* (Rhubarb! 2003) and *In Europe The Ceilings Are Very High* at the Tarragon Theatre-hosted Paprika Festival, in 2004. Another play, *The Problem With Being A Pond*, was Tarragon Theatre's 2003 Under Twenties Playwriting Contest winner. Daniel was the inaugural playwright-in-residence at the Paprika Festival.

Daniel has acted at Toronto's Tarragon Theatre, with Modern Times Stage Company, and in a handful of new plays at the SummerWorks Festival. Film and TV credits include work with Alliance Atlantis, CBC, CTV, Global, NBC and Walt Disney Films. A native of Thornhill, Ontario, Daniel currently lives in Toronto, where he is a member of the Tarragon's Playwrights Unit.

For my family.

In Full Light was first presented in August 2007 by Tango Co. as part of the SummerWorks Theatre Festival, at the Tarragon Theatre mainspace, Toronto, with the following company:

CLAIRE	Monica Dottor
BEN	Tom Barnett
LEON	David Ferry
LOLA	Gina Wilkinson
MARSHALL	Brendan Gall

Directed and designed by Natasha Mytnowych.
Dramaturgy by Iris Turcott.
Lighting by André du Toit and Natasha Mytnowych.
Sound and music design by Lyon Smith.
Costume design by Naomi Skwarna.
Choreography by Monica Dottor.
Stage managed by Jennifer Dowding and Joy Lachica.

In Full Light was the recipient of the 2007 SummerWorks Festival's Contra Guys Award for Outstanding New Play.

In Full Light was developed in part through the Canadian Stage Company's play development programme.

Characters

CLAIRE, 15
LEON, 45
BEN, 42, Claire's father
LOLA, 38, Ben's wife
MARSHALL, 19, who lives across the street

Notes on Punctuation

... marks a silence.
/ marks a place where the line following is spoken early, creating overlap.

Acknowledgements

Much gratitude to Natasha Mytnowych, Iris Turcott, and our stellar cast and crew for the SummerWorks production; to the artists who were involved at an earlier stage of this play's development: Mark Ellis, Randy Hughson, Andy McKim, Matthew Edison, Sarah Orenstein; to my friends who read the play and said stuff to me about it: Kevin Shea, Wade Bogert-O'Brien, Naomi Skwarna; and to Al Moritz for his poem. Thank you.

Then a few things will follow
from these first conditions: women
singing in full light and at dusk
before reflecting water;
and some way to live together
that is not a scandal and a shame.
　　　　—A. F. Moritz, "What They Prayed For"

IN FULL LIGHT

A rush of air. A screech of brakes. CLAIRE is splayed out violently, unnaturally, in the middle of the road. She's still. Watching her, around her, are BEN, LOLA, MARSHALL and LEON. Each of them is isolated, alone. CLAIRE shifts. She shifts again. Is she injured or is she posing?

CLAIRE   How should I be? Like this?

As though both arms were broken.

Or like this?

Tongue out, fingers up her nose, legs twisted out of place.

Oh fuck me. So ridiculous. I'm dying, I'm gonna die, like for sure probably, and all I can think about is whether you thought I was beautiful when I flew up the windshield.

LEON is in distress. BEN turns to him.

LEON   I can't even begin to understand—

BEN   So what happened, she / just—

LEON   Just stopped walking all of a sudden in the middle of the street, I slammed on my brakes, I wasn't really even going that fast but I guess—are you all right?

BEN   I'm fine, finish what you're saying.

LEON   I'm really so sorry, I can't tell you—

BEN   Finish what you're saying.

LEON   No please, listen to me, I'm really a low shit, making excuses for myself right after I've, I've—I'm sure you don't want to chit-chat with me. I'm sure you'd rather hit me.

BEN   Hit you? I don't want to hit you.

LEON   I would want to. In your position. Somebody hurt my daughter, I'd want to hit him.

LOLA places a hand on BEN's shoulder. BEN turns to her. LEON is gone.

LOLA   So did you?

BEN   Excuse me?

LOLA   Did you hit him.

BEN   Are you kidding?

LOLA   ...

BEN   No. No, of course I didn't hit him. Why would I hit him?

CLAIRE is in the hospital. The beep of a monitor.

CLAIRE   Invisibility. Absolute invisibility. It's the only explanation. My dad comes into the room, he sits beside the bed, he talks to himself, he gets up and leaves. He doesn't see me. He can kiss me on the cheek without seeing me. And all these doctors buzzing around, calling my name but not meaning me by it—can they see me? Maybe they're blind, all these blind doctors moving blindly through this hospital where all the patients can see. And you—would you be able to see me if you were here? Why aren't you here? Haven't you heard?

LOLA is on MARSHALL's front porch.

MARSHALL   Heard what?

LOLA   She was hit by a car.

MARSHALL   Oh.

LOLA   Oh?

MARSHALL   I mean yeah. I know. I mean I knew. Before just now.

LOLA   You did. Good. And so I was wondering, you're always at your window there, doing your bird thing—

MARSHALL   Oh not *always*, just, like, sometimes—

LOLA   And we've been trying to figure out exactly how this terrible thing happened, how she managed to get herself—

MARSHALL   You want to know if I saw it?

LOLA   Did you see it?

MARSHALL   What's it worth to you?

LOLA   ...

MARSHALL   Kidding. I'm kidding, that's a joke, I'm sorry, I, uh, I guess this isn't the right time, is it? Yeah. Yes. I'll be serious now.

LOLA   I'm not sure what it's worth to me. Why don't you tell me first and then we can work something out?

MARSHALL   ...where's, uh... where's... your husband?

LOLA   At the hospital.

MARSHALL   ...yeah. Um. So like. What you wanted to... know. She ran out into the road. She stopped. He kept going. He hit her. He got out of his car, he pulled out his cell phone, he called the ambulance. Ambulance arrived, ambulance left, he went with. That's all I saw.

LOLA   Thanks.

MARSHALL   Please.

LOLA   I hope you're still drawing.

MARSHALL   Oh. Yes. I am. Sometimes. It's cyclical. But I have to waste eight or nine hours for every hour of work I get done.

LOLA   Well. I'm sorry to interrupt your procrastination.

MARSHALL   Oh. No. You're... welcome.

LOLA   ...

MARSHALL   Do you / wanna—?

LOLA   I'd better / go.

MARSHALL   Yeah. Yes.

LOLA   Take / care.

MARSHALL   And you.

> *CLAIRE is in the hospital, BEN seated beside her.*

CLAIRE   ...did he say he was sorry?

BEN   ...he said he was sorry.

CLAIRE   ...so...

BEN   ...so... I'm not sure... the important... the most important thing is that you get better...

CLAIRE   ...yeah.

BEN   ...I'm going to... I'm not sure exactly.

CLAIRE   You don't need to sue him or get him arrested or anything, Daddy.

BEN   He wasn't drinking.

CLAIRE   You don't have to do anything. It's okay.

BEN   It was an accident. And... you know I feel... but it was an / accident.

CLAIRE   I feel better already.

> *LEON appears, leads BEN away. A reception area in the hospital.*

LEON   That's good to hear, I mean jeez, I've just been thinking and thinking about it, how can you stop, you know, but I didn't think it was the proper thing to go up to her room and express my contrition if you can understand / where I'm coming from—

BEN   Of course, no, I don't think that's / necessary—

LEON   But I do feel that her well-being is my, in a way I mean, my responsibility, or that, well, that this is my fault, I guess is the bottom of it, this is all my fault, and I'm not sleeping, that's not your problem of course but I can't sleep anymore, haven't been able to now for two weeks, so...

BEN   ...

LEON   I feel the need to compensate you for the, the situation I've put you and your family in, and I feel like me sitting around saying "sorry, sorry" doesn't cut it.

BEN   Oh, well, that's, I appreciate that, but there's really no need to.... What exactly are you talking about?

LEON   I wrote you a cheque.

BEN   ...but you know that I can't—I can't—I mean I couldn't—because— that's very generous of you but I wouldn't want you to find yourself in financial... I would feel very awkward about...

LEON   You're worried I can't afford it?

BEN   Can you?

LEON   I'm not sleeping, Benjamin.

BEN   Just Ben is fine.

LEON   I want to sleep, Ben. I'm being straight with you. I want to feel okay again. I want to enjoy eating meals again. When I shave in the morning I want to be able to look at myself in the mirror.

BEN   I'm not sure if money will change any of that.

LEON   Maybe not. You ever have insomnia, Ben?

BEN   ...

LEON   What do you do? You can't sleep so you what, you get up, you go to the kitchen, mix yourself a drink, what do you drink? scotch, you close your eyes. You sit on the couch, you watch the TV, you watch the coloured bars on stations that are out of service, what else? you take long walks in the street maybe, you walk in the shadows because you don't want to be seen but every time a car passes you hope it'll stop and a friend will get out, someone who'll be a comfort, someone you can trust.

BEN This is a little besides the point, don't you think?

LEON How's your marriage?

BEN What?

LEON Healthy? Yeah? I'm curious.

BEN That's kind of a personal question, don't you—

LEON I'm sorry, is that not—?

BEN My marriage is fine. Thanks.

LEON I'm not married, myself.

BEN Okay.

LEON Is your wife Claire's mother?

BEN Excuse me—?

LEON I'm sorry, is that not a polite / question?

BEN A polite—I guess that depends what you consider—I don't think— why would you ask that? No. I don't know. No, I—no, my wife is not Claire's mother, Claire's mother is in Montreal.

LEON Is that complicated?

BEN Not really, no, but—sorry, you'll have to excuse me, but it's very strange for me to be talking about this with you, considering the, the circumstances of our…

LEON Yeah, I guess—

BEN So to be sitting here talking about my ex with you, I never talk about my ex, frankly I'd rather talk about crabs, and here we are—

LEON You can't always choose when and how you make a friend.

BEN I don't think I'm the type of person who makes a lot of friends.

LEON I'm the same way. I've got a lot of respect for you, you know.

BEN Okay. Thanks.

LEON Got a lot of respect for your situation, what you do, you know what I'm driving at? you're a *family* man, you live for people other than yourself, even when we're sitting here and I offer you this large sum of money I can see you thinking not just about yourself, like a lot of people, but also your family, how will this help them, how will this change their respect for you, all that. I can see that.

BEN I won't accept a handout from a stranger.

LEON It's not a handout, it's reparations.

BEN I'm thinking about it.

LEON Don't think too much.

> *He fishes a folded cheque from his pocket and places it in BEN's hands.*

BEN ...that's a lot of money.

LEON I do okay for myself.

BEN What can I say? What should I say to you?

LEON Don't say anything.

> *CLAIRE is at her bedroom window.*

CLAIRE Ornithology. The study of birds. The study of watching. Waiting and watching. Eight every morning.

> *MARSHALL comes to his window with binoculars and notepad. He and CLAIRE can't hear each other.*

I once heard you telling Lola:

MARSHALL It's calming. Like—

CLAIRE Watching people. It's like watching people in the early morning—

MARSHALL Only with birds the whole thing is simpler, because when you watch people you think:

CLAIRE I need to understand—

MARSHALL To understand, just to understand, how does it feel to be the man who delivers the water for our cooler, how does it feel to be the woman carrying her baby to the clinic at dawn—?

CLAIRE But with birds, watching birds—

MARSHALL It's much simpler, because I accept that I will never know what it is to be a bird, so I don't feel that endless responsibility to understand why the thing that I'm watching does what it does, and I can just—

CLAIRE Watch.

MARSHALL And record what's beautiful on paper, neat and logical.

CLAIRE You pretend you're oblivious.

MARSHALL I never learned the real names of birds. I can recognize a robin, a hawk, maybe a seagull. The rest I've created names for myself. Johnny-of-the-afternoon. Blue-who-heads-to-the-sea.

CLAIRE   But I've been so *obvious*. You must know. You must know everything. But if you know why do you just *torture* me like this?

MARSHALL   Long-who-kisses-lawns-and-leaves. Wide-wings-leaving-on-wind-tomorrow.

CLAIRE   One of these days I'm going to knock on your door and say something to you, and then we'll actually have spoken, and what're you gonna do then, huh? Will you confess everything, you love me too and have delayed so long because you're a horrible person but you want to be better and can I teach you to be a better person? Will you say that?

MARSHALL   A chart for each bird, patterns of behaviour, quirks, moments of strange beauty. Morley-who-sings-away-seagulls. Lola-who-comes-to-make-chit-chat.

CLAIRE   If you haven't come to see how I'm feeling by tomorrow I'm going to knock on your door and tell you.

MARSHALL   Claire-at-the-window-hiding.

CLAIRE   And if you can't see me I'll murder you invisibly.

MARSHALL   A chart for each bird, patterns of behaviour, quirks, moments of strange beauty.

CLAIRE   If you don't come by tomorrow. Tomorrow—

> *Suddenly an insistent knocking at the door. CLAIRE goes to the door, opens it. There's MARSHALL. A long moment. She's staring. Then she can't meet his eye.*

MARSHALL   ...oh hi.

CLAIRE   ...

MARSHALL   Um. You were hit by a car.

CLAIRE   ...uh-huh.

MARSHALL   That's real bad news. Sorry.

CLAIRE   ...yeah sorry. Yeah. I mean yeah, okay. Don't be sorry or anything.

MARSHALL   So, uh, you have my deepest, my most sincere, um...

CLAIRE   Yeah?

MARSHALL   Condolences?

CLAIRE   ...oh. Thanks. Okay bye.

MARSHALL   Claire?

CLAIRE   Yes?

MARSHALL   No, nothing, I just wanted to make sure I had your name right.

CLAIRE   Claire.

MARSHALL   Yeah, I know.

CLAIRE   You must be smart. And your name, it starts with like an *N* or an… *L*…?

MARSHALL   It's Marshall.

CLAIRE   Oh, okay. Does anyone ever call you "Fire Marshall"?

MARSHALL   All the time.

CLAIRE   My condolences.

MARSHALL   So you were in the hospital, huh?

CLAIRE   Yeah. The hospital for the sighted.

MARSHALL   Huh?

CLAIRE   I dunno. Yeah.

MARSHALL   So… that sucks.

CLAIRE   Yeah.

MARSHALL   …

CLAIRE   Um, don't you have anywhere to be, now, like aren't you in school or something?

MARSHALL   Oh. Well, I graduated.

CLAIRE   University?

MARSHALL   It's June.

CLAIRE   So in June you get to just bum around and be a jerk.

MARSHALL   …

CLAIRE   Hello?

MARSHALL   …

CLAIRE   What is wrong with you?

LOLA   Claire, I can't find my blouse with the stripes.

        LOLA comes up behind her.

CLAIRE   I stole it.

LOLA   Thanks, thanks for the help. Hi Marshall, how are you?

MARSHALL   I don't know.

LOLA   Sorry to hear that.

MARSHALL   Yeah. Yes. True. So... feel better.

>   *He goes.*

LOLA   That's a very nice-looking kid.

CLAIRE   Oh my God. Can you be even a little bit serious? I'd rather sleep with a pine tree.

LOLA   You shouldn't be sleeping with anyone.

CLAIRE   No, I don't know where your blouse is.

LOLA   Fine, fine, I've really gotta get—you don't hate me, do you?

CLAIRE   Not at all.

LOLA   Don't hate me. I'm really not worth hating.

>   *BEN is in his office. The phone rings. He picks up.*

BEN   Hello—?

LEON   Why should a chemist be so hard to reach, I ask myself.

BEN   Is this—? Who is this?

LEON   This is Leon, you don't recognize my voice?

BEN   Leon... from the—?

LEON   Sure, Leon, you know other Leons? maybe you know other Leons but I'd imagine I might be quite a large figure in your thinking if you know what it is I'm saying—

BEN   Right, yes, Leon, yes, so what is it, what's going on?

LEON   What is it a chemist does exactly? is it dangerous? If you put the wrong thing in the wrong bottle, know what I mean? seems like it could be a real bad—

BEN   Leon is there something you want to say to me—

LEON   I'm sorry, sorry, listen to me, I run off at the mouth, but I, look, I can't do it like this, we've gotta meet, can you meet me?

BEN   I'm at work, Leon.

LEON   Of course, well aren't I just a son of a bitch, I'll try you another time, sorry to have interrupted, really, I mean I shouldn't expect a guy to be always on call for me just because I know him a little, that's all right, that's all right, I'm fine, I'm okay, I'll try you later.

He hangs up abruptly.

CLAIRE is at her bedroom window. She's scribbling on a piece of paper. Then she rips the paper up. And again. And again.

CLAIRE   He knows everything.

MARSHALL is at his bedroom window. Binoculars.

He thinks because he's old and has those dark jeans he can just do whatever the frig he wants. "So I heard you were hit by a car!" But you never said a word to me.

MARSHALL   She's seen me. She didn't / have to say—

CLAIRE   You didn't say *an-y-thing*—

MARSHALL   It was an accusation: each little tip of her hip that she does like that: pervert, weirdo, creep.

CLAIRE   You were thinking, "She's pathetic, she's silly, she's ugly, and I have to make sure she *knows* that."

MARSHALL   I don't want to get any closer than this. We'd have nothing to say to each other. She's too happy. Too optimistic.

CLAIRE   And you want to kill me, your deepest darkest desire I *know* you is to see me suffer at the teeth of wild animals who eat hair too and to see me fall from a poetic height and die. You wish no afterlife for me so that when I'm gone from the earth I'll be gone also from conception, from eternity, forever. That way I can't haunt you.

MARSHALL   I'm afraid of changing her.

CLAIRE   I am going to write the filthiest words for you, I am going to write you words so filthy, so awful you'll think how horrible it is that people exist who can hate so much.

MARSHALL   I'm afraid of fouling something pure.

CLAIRE is writing.

CLAIRE   "You are going to roll in the filth of pigs who sweat and shit at the same time and the pigs are going to step on your face and then you'll be no less pretty but that's before the pigs *eat* you."

MARSHALL   No. Better like this. Dependable.

CLAIRE   "Tomorrow a big man is going to kick you in the balls and you'll say 'Why?' and then he'll kick you in the balls again and your balls will fall off and at this point you'll get the idea to run but then he'll hit you with a steel bar and you'll be only a little less pretty then but that's still before he *eats* you."

MARSHALL   Uncomplicated.

CLAIRE   "Suck my cock."

> *The phone rings. We hear the others but see only CLAIRE. She picks up.*

...is it you?

LEON   ...can I speak to Ben, please?

CLAIRE   Oh. Who's this?

LEON   Who's this? I'm a good friend.

CLAIRE   You've got the wrong number. My dad doesn't have friends.

LEON   ...

CLAIRE   Hang on, hang on. Dad! For you.

BEN   Hello?

LEON   Come outside.

BEN   Excuse me—who—Leon?

LEON   Come outside, Ben.

BEN   ...where are you?

LEON   It's an emergency. I wouldn't do this if it wasn't. Come outside.

BEN   Where are you, Leon?

LEON   I'm across the street from your house.

> *We see BEN and LEON, standing on opposite sides of the street. LEON holds a small duffle.*

BEN   ...why didn't you knock?

LEON   ...if your daughter...

BEN   ...listen, Leon. If you're in some kind of trouble I sympathize with you but I don't want you bringing that here where my family—

LEON   The trouble is I don't have any money.

> *He crosses the street and meets BEN. BEN glances behind him to his house. His windows.*

BEN   You don't have any money.

LEON   Yeah, that would be my problem, I'm broke. I have nothing.

BEN   But you told me you had a... I don't understand.

LEON   Neither do I, life is strange, you know? First thing I hit a girl with my truck, next thing I lose my job, but oh, whoopsie, I've just given away all my savings to someone I know fuck all / about, excuse me—

BEN   No excuse *me*, what?

LEON   Sure, you think I just had six thousand dollars tucked under my bed in case of some crisis of conscience? *no*, Ben, and that's okay, you know, I'm an adult, I can make decisions and live with them, but the problem is now I have *nothing*, no money, no job—

BEN   Hang on, hang on, wait, that money was all your savings?

LEON   I smashed the piggy bank.

BEN   But… but then I can't understand… no, but why would you—

LEON   Because I'm not a bad person, Ben. Because I think about people other than myself.

BEN   You know there's selfless and then there's ridiculous.

LEON   You find me ridiculous?

BEN   So what is it you want? you didn't call me up just to—

LEON   I don't like this new tone, Ben, guys can still be friends when things get difficult.

BEN   Leon let me be clear, and I don't want to·be rude and I don't want to hurt your feelings, but considering everything I don't think of us as friends in the way you mean. So… I'm sorry, I just…

LEON   Well. It's a shame you feel that way.

BEN   I want to be honest with you.

LEON   You're very honest, I respect that about you.

BEN   Okay, so that's all we have to talk about, right? I'm sorry about your situation but—

LEON   The thing is I need the money back, Ben.

BEN   The money you gave me?

LEON   That's the only money there is.

BEN   But you… I don't feel comfortable with the idea that—but you gave it to me.

LEON   Yes, I know, and now I need it back.

BEN   It's gone.

LEON   It's gone. Where has it gone? You spent six thousand dollars in two weeks?

BEN   It's gone. You gave it to me and I used it.

LEON   Only natural.

BEN   What did you expect me to do with it? you hand me a cheque, you *insist*—

LEON   I never insisted—

BEN   —you *insist* I take it, so that you can sleep at night, I take it, I spend it. You have no reason to be angry or surprised—

LEON   I'm not surprised, I'm not angry, I'm just *asking*. I'm asking you to do me a favour, I'm in need and I'm *asking*, I'm not demanding, I'm not shouting, I'm just asking you to remember that I wasn't a bad guy to you when I could've been—

BEN   That's entirely different—

LEON   —okay it's different, you're right, I'm just telling you where I'm at now and asking if you can help a guy out. I don't have anywhere to sleep. I don't have anywhere to sleep or anything to eat and I'm asking you to help a guy out.

BEN   ...

LEON   You're just gonna walk back into your house? You're gonna walk back into your warm, comfortable house and leave me standing here?

BEN   ...

LEON   I know I deserve it. I know that's what I deserve, man. Make no mistake.

BEN   ...

LEON   I have nowhere to go, Ben. I have nowhere to sleep.

BEN   ...

LEON   You have a couch?

BEN   Pardon me?

LEON   The money's gone, I understand, only natural, but if I could lay my bones on your couch for a few days that'd really help me lots.

BEN   I really don't think I... my family is there.

LEON   Just a few days, Ben. Just till I can get things straightened out. I'll figure out how to get hold of some cash. Just need a bit of time.

BEN ...I don't think I can.

LEON ...

BEN Really. It's not a good idea. I'm sorry.

LEON ...

BEN I'm sorry.

> *LEON turns and starts slowly to walk away. A moment.*

...hold on.

> *LEON stops.*

...just... but... but just for a few days.

LEON That's it.

BEN ...and... and... absolutely no later than the end of the week.

LEON Absolutely.

BEN ...all right.

LEON That's very generous of you, Ben.

BEN ...well. I wouldn't want to be the kind of guy who...

> *Darkness falls around them. Soon we can see only MARSHALL in the window, CLAIRE's note in his hand.*

LEON You're exactly like me.

> *LEON and LOLA are in the kitchen, LOLA holding a cup of coffee.*

LOLA Oh, yeah?

LEON No milk, no cream, a little sugar.

LOLA Would you like a cup?

LEON Oh no, just saying.

LOLA Any luck with the paper, did you find anything?

LEON Sure, sure, lots of jobs out there, trouble is I'm not really qualified for anything. Spent most of my life in the merchant marine. Most of my working life. Signed up when I was fourteen. I'd seen more of the world at twenty-five than most people will see if they live to be a hundred. Six continents, all kinds of labour, manual labour. I've been kidnapped for ransom and held at gunpoint twice. I've known countless ports of call and the people in them. That's a hard-working, honest life.

LOLA   I think it's admirable that you've done things that excite you. The merchant marine sounds adventurous—

LEON   Yeah shit, excuse me, but that's a load of you know what; adventure is what it is at seventeen. By twenty, make no mistake, it's work. Certainly there's no pride there for me now. Do you think I've told your husband that that's how I've spent the better part of my life?

LOLA   You haven't told Ben—?

LEON   No I did not tell your husband that I spent years and years in a community of men with a reputation for extreme misogyny and violence. No I did not.

LOLA   He's more compassionate than you think.

LEON   He would throw me out of your house. Politely, of course. But he would throw me out of your house. And he's right, that's exactly what he should do, because he's got you and his daughter here and he's got to think about you first. Your safety.

LOLA   That's really absurd, Leon.

LEON   Is it?

LOLA   ...the merchant marine, huh? I've never met anyone before who's done that for a living. It was really that bad?

LEON   Well no, it wasn't bad, but like anywhere else you had a mix of honest men and men who'd take a knife to your hand in the night for the rings on your fingers. Often the same man contained both possibilities.

LOLA   I would never take a knife to your hand for the rings on your fingers. Neither would Ben. So you can sleep easy here.

LEON   Thanks. That's very kind of you to say. But then you and Ben don't have any need of rings.

LOLA   We're honest besides.

LEON   Your husband married quite a remarkable woman.

LOLA   Yeah, his first wife. Anyway, if you're okay here I'm going to head out for a while—

LEON   No, I never married, myself.

LOLA   Too many ports of call?

LEON   Oh no, no. Just never married. I was engaged once.

LOLA   Uh-huh.

LEON   Oh yeah. Yeah, yeah. Once upon a time. It didn't work out.

LOLA   I'm sorry.

LEON   She decided I was too dependent.

LOLA   Were you?

LEON   ...it's good to be around people again, you know? You spend too much time alone, you begin to lose your bearings. My apartment wasn't very big. Even the windows were narrow.

LOLA   You can also be alone in a bed you're sharing once the lights go out.

The lights go out. Night.

MARSHALL crosses to CLAIRE's house and leaves a slip of paper in the handle of her front door. CLAIRE snaps on her flashlight, leaves her house, retrieves and reads his note.

CLAIRE   "You eat Chinese food? Maybe we should go eat Chinese food together. If you want. You know where I live. M."

She's still a moment. Then she rips his note into pieces, blows her nose with the pieces, and stomps them underfoot.

This is how the universe laughs at me. I tell him I love him, I use words that aren't as pretty and stuff but still I tell him, and he asks me if I want *Chinese food*? There is a name for that, that is *cruelty*, he could say no, I don't love you, but oh no! he wants to cause me pain. Probably very few people make themselves vulnerable like that for him so when he sees the opportunity, *wham!* he grabs it. The fucking cunt-faced cocksucker son of a bitch.

With her flashlight she finds a large rock. She picks it up and shuffles it between her hands. It's not light.

Fuck with somebody else, asswipe.

She wings the rock into MARSHALL's bedroom window and runs back to the safety of her house as the window shatters.

MARSHALL wakes up. He sees the window in pieces. He stumbles forward and finds the rock among the shards. He picks it up, looks at it, tosses it back and forth between his hands. On his face is a look of pure wonder.

MARSHALL   Look at that. Look at that.

He's smiling like an ecstatic standing for the first time in holy light. He can't move.

No one has ever...

He stands in the window frame, where the glass used to be. His face is blanched a ghostly white by the light of the moon.

CLAIRE returns to her house, closing the front door soundlessly. The beam of her flashlight catches on LEON's face. She jumps, makes a noise, startled. Hastily she snaps the flashlight off. For a moment there's complete silence and darkness.

LEON Sorry I scared you.

She snaps the flashlight back on. LEON is sitting alone in the living room. With wariness she approaches him, lights him. Then impulsively she sits down beside him. Their faces are lit by her flashlight beam.

CLAIRE What are you doing?

LEON Sitting.

CLAIRE Just sitting?

LEON Listening to the night. There was a crash.

CLAIRE A cat knocked over a garbage can.

LEON Sounded like glass breaking.

CLAIRE There was glass inside the garbage can.

LEON Why are you walking around with a flashlight—?

CLAIRE Hey, this is my house, I can do that if I want, okay?

LEON You can do anything you want.

CLAIRE Fucking right.

LEON You're very polite.

CLAIRE Love has made a monster of me.

LEON Love. .

CLAIRE Love. You wouldn't know anything about it.

LEON You think I've never been in love.

CLAIRE Not the same kind. I mean a scratch his face, vomit in his shoes, throw his liver to the dogs kind of love. You can't touch that kind of love.

LEON I once threw a woman I loved down a flight of stairs.

CLAIRE ...really?

LEON Sure.

CLAIRE   Why?

LEON   She stopped loving me. I still loved her.

CLAIRE   So, what do you do to someone you hate?

LEON   ...sorry, sweetheart, I don't think I understand your question.

CLAIRE   ...you don't make me feel safe at all.

LEON   Am I supposed to?

CLAIRE   You're old. Most old people do.

LEON   What would I have to do to make you feel safe?

CLAIRE   Not remind me of me.

LEON   It's late. Shouldn't you get a little sleep?

CLAIRE   ...we're not kind, people like us, you realize?

LEON   Speak for yourself. I'm a very kind person.

CLAIRE   I'm not a kind person. But I want to be. I think I do. I *want* to want to be.

LEON   Whoever told you it's to your advantage to be kind was lying through his teeth.

CLAIRE   Sooner or later he's going to throw you out of our house.

LEON   Maybe. But why do you think so?

CLAIRE   Because of the things that are in your head. I've seen you.

>   *CLAIRE's flashlight snaps off. Darkness.*

LOLA   Claire? Is that... oh. Hi. Can't sleep?

LEON   I rarely sleep.

>   *Sound of a window curtain pushed aside. Moonlight seeps in.*

LOLA   You're welcome to turn on the TV...

LEON   Don't like late-night television. Thanks.

LOLA   Whatever you like. I just heard a noise and thought I'd better...

LEON   Lola.

LOLA   ...goodnight, Leon.

LEON   I try to live honestly.

LOLA   I know that, Leon. Hope you can get some sleep. I'll see you in the morning.

LEON   Wait.

LOLA   …

LEON   Wait.

LOLA   …

LEON   I want to tell you this outright, I don't want to play games, or, or do those things people do, I'm not interested. And I'm sorry to approach you like this, to back you into a corner such as it is, but I'm very afraid right now, I've got just lots and lots of fear, right now, and this is how I've got to do it, forgive me.

LOLA   …you've been a guest in our home, Leon.

LEON   I know that, I know, frankly I know exactly what you're going to say, and that's fine, that's just fine. I think you are a remarkable woman and truly and fully unappreciated where you are at this moment, and I look at your life and I think, how sad that is, how boring it must be, how lonely. You're an outsider in your own house. Is this an accurate picture I'm painting?

LOLA   …you don't understand.

LEON   No, really I don't understand, I don't understand why a woman like you, beautiful, intelligent—why you keep on going this way, when you could be so much happier—what is it? is it comfort that keeps you going like this, familiarity, routine—?

LOLA   I don't have to explain myself to you.

LEON   This is a simple request I have, just hear me out. I know it's dark and we're alone and that's a potentially threatening or uncomfortable position for you to be in, and me too. This is what I want to do. I want to put my hand in your hair. I may touch your face. That's all I want. If you're not interested in my idea I will respect that and leave you alone. I know you're a faithful wife, I wouldn't want to change that. I want only to make you aware of your options.

LOLA   …

LEON   You're not saying anything. That's fine. That's wise. You're guilty of nothing.

> *Quite tenderly he runs his hand through her hair. She flinches. She pulls away. He looks at her. He places, again, his hand in her hair. She flinches. But she doesn't pull away. He cups and strokes the side of her face.*

LOLA   Leon…

LEON   ...shh. Not necessary.

LOLA   ...I'm not a weak person. You can't imagine what strength I have in me.

LEON   I won't kiss you unless you ask me to.

LOLA   I love my husband.

LEON   He's a very good man. I respect him very much.

LOLA   Clearly not.

LEON   I have tremendous admiration and respect for you. It saddens me that you have your eyes closed like this. You're afraid of loneliness. Okay. So am I. So is he. I can see all of you.

LOLA   My life is with my husband.

LEON   I won't kiss you unless in no uncertain terms you ask me to.

LOLA ̇ I won't.

LEON   Then we can stand here like this all night and I'll be perfectly happy.

LOLA   ...

LEON   So will you.

> *She doesn't move.*

> *Elsewhere: a pebble raps against a window. And again. A light comes on. CLAIRE looks out the window, then goes to the front door, takes a breath, and opens it for MARSHALL.*

MARSHALL   So I got your message.

CLAIRE   ...

MARSHALL   So I got your message—?

CLAIRE   I didn't send you a message.

MARSHALL   Oh. But like, it's—okay fine, forget it.

CLAIRE   ...

MARSHALL   So were you sleeping just now or something or what—?

CLAIRE   It wasn't a message.

MARSHALL   ...

CLAIRE   It was a rock.

MARSHALL   Oh. Yeah I know.

CLAIRE   So listen, I'm sorry, okay? Are you gonna ask me to like pay for the—

MARSHALL   No, no, I just wanted to tell you that I appreciated it.

CLAIRE   Appreciated it how?

MARSHALL   Just… I dunno. Take it at face value.

CLAIRE   Oh. So… you're welcome?

MARSHALL   …so what's going on, like what were you doing just now when I came, like with your life I mean?

CLAIRE   It's three in the morning.

MARSHALL   Sure, sure, still.

CLAIRE   I was sleeping.

MARSHALL   Yeah okay. Sleeping. Right. But you're not sleeping anymore, so, uh, what do you wanna do?

CLAIRE   …

MARSHALL   I mean it's okay if you just want to go back to sleep. I can go home. I don't live far.

CLAIRE   …you're making fun of me.

MARSHALL   What? No, no. I'm… I don't know, I'm talking.

CLAIRE   …you're not fucking with my head?

MARSHALL   I don't think so.

CLAIRE   …it's three in the morning and you're asking me what I want to do?

MARSHALL   Uh-huh, yeah, I think so.

CLAIRE   …I want to see my house.

MARSHALL   Turn around.

CLAIRE   I want to see my house like you see my house. I want to see my bedroom.

> *A moment. He turns, motions for her to follow. They enter his house. His bedroom. They look out his window.*

…can't see much.

MARSHALL   You're not using binoculars. You want to look through the binoculars?

> *She takes one of his hands and clasps it.*

...ah, I see, well that's not a binocular, actually...

CLAIRE   ...

He slips his hand away from hers.

MARSHALL   I... I'm kinda...

CLAIRE   Oh fuck this.

MARSHALL   I'm sorry, I'm just—

CLAIRE   Yeah.

MARSHALL   No listen—

CLAIRE   Yeah, yeah that's what I thought—

MARSHALL   But it's not, like, you, it's, it's me, or it's girls, in general—

CLAIRE   Right, right, so you're gay—

MARSHALL   No, no unfortunately not gay either, I just don't get it, I'm sorry, just not programmed that way, I don't even understand how two people can even like each other enough to—

CLAIRE   Well fuck you too—

MARSHALL   You don't understand—

CLAIRE   Oh I understand perfectly, you think I'm too weird for you and I look ugly up close—

MARSHALL   No, I'm—

CLAIRE   Oh please, please! don't make it worse! I got hit by a car for your sake you cocksucker and all you have to say to me is "I'm just not programmed that way"? You *asshole*—!

MARSHALL   For my sake—?

CLAIRE   Yeah, sure, why do think I was standing in the middle of the road, huh!? I was coming to see you, I was coming to *make fucking contact* and I looked up at your window apparently for just a second too long—

MARSHALL   I don't know if you can really blame me for that—

CLAIRE   Well I do! Murderer!

She runs.

Elsewhere:

BEN   Get out of my house.

BEN and LEON are alone.

You take your bag and you get out. Don't say anything. You get out.

LEON You don't understand—

BEN I don't need to.

LEON Yes you do need to, Ben, you need to cool down and hear me out, this is no way to treat a friend—

BEN Don't, no, no no no *don't*, please, would you please not use that word with me, would you please *get* your fucking bag and go somewhere I can't see you—

LEON You really need to relax, Ben.

BEN Fuck you, get out.

LEON I don't appreciate that.

BEN Fuck you get out fuck you get out get the fuck out of my house, do you understand?

LEON This is very unlike you, Ben. If your wife and kid saw you—

BEN No, sorry, I don't think you understand the situation. You were a guest in my house, I didn't know you, I didn't *trust* you, *you were a guest in my house*. You took advantage. And now you are no longer welcome. Is that more clear?

LEON I never touched your wife without her permission.

BEN …

LEON What, you gonna hit me? Hit me.

BEN …

LEON No? No. Okay. No. You know, Ben, I look hard at you and all I see is a sad little shit who's spent so much time hiding in the office he's afraid to fuck his wife.

BEN …get out of my house.

LEON With pleasure. Just as soon as we settle accounts.

BEN …oh no no no, you son of a bitch, I don't owe you a—

LEON Tell me, Ben, why do women flock to men like you, men without spine? Your wife's far too good for you.

BEN Maybe. But she's far too good for you too.

LEON Oh yes, oh absolutely, your whole family is too good for me, your house, your little garden. Much too good for me. Cheque please.

BEN Do I have to forcibly remove you from my house?

LEON   Is that a rhetorical question?

BEN   Get out.

LEON   No no, I liked that other option, why don't you "forcibly remove me from your house," that sounded interesting.

BEN   Do I have to call the police?

LEON   What's that going to do, Ben? They'll make me go, but do you think I'll leave you alone, your family, your little garden? If that's what you think we really aren't as close as I thought—

BEN   You son of a bitch, if you so much as look at my family—

LEON   You'll get really angry, right? your face will get all red just like now, right?

BEN   ...

LEON   Are you going to settle up with me or not?

> *BEN spits in LEON's face.*

Ah. Ah yes. That's what I thought. And you know what, Ben? That's just fine. I've taken a security measure. You hear this?

> *He shakes his bag. Something rattles inside.*

LEON   Because I've got no legal way of collecting what I'm owed I've resorted to taking some things of value from your bedroom. I've put a considerable amount of your wife's jewellery into my bag, along with a couple of your nicer watches and some cash that was on the dresser. I regret having to be so crude about it but that's the position you put me in with your unwillingness to share the wealth.

BEN   Are you joking?

LEON   Do you think I'm joking?

BEN   You're out of your mind. You know I won't let you leave the house with my stuff in your bag.

LEON   But that's the truly amazing thing. You will. You almost certainly will. Because what's going to happen, Ben? we'll grapple with the bag, we'll struggle, you'll pull and pull, but I'm a pretty strong guy, no? and chances are I'll maintain my hold and you'll have to decide, what are you prepared to do? Are you gonna kill me? Are you gonna knock me unconscious? And I think in your honest, miserable heart of hearts the answer is no.

BEN   ...

LEON   What are you prepared to do?

BEN   Have you not a shred of—?

LEON   What. Are you. Prepared. To do.

BEN   ...

LEON   That's what I thought.

BEN   ...

LEON   It was nice knowing you, Ben.

> *He leaves BEN standing in the doorway. BEN does not move. LOLA appears beside him.*
>
> *They're in their bedroom. She touches his chest. He won't look at her.*

BEN   ...you don't need to say anything.

> *She touches his face.*

...I... I trust you. I trust you. I'm not a jealous...

LOLA   ...why won't you look at me?

BEN   I'm looking at you.

> *She moves her hand up his thigh. She touches his crotch. He's still; but in a moment jerks abruptly away from her.*

I'm sorry.

LOLA   Don't be sorry.

BEN   I'm sorry.

LOLA   Ben...

BEN   ...

LOLA   Look at me, please? What are you thinking?

BEN   ...did you...

LOLA   ...did I what?

BEN   ...did you find him... do you find that type of... did you find him romantic?

LOLA   ...no. Not romantic.

BEN   Exciting?

LOLA   What?

BEN   Did you find him exciting? did you think he was more alive somehow than I am or...

LOLA   No, Ben, no, I didn't, I found him—

BEN   Interesting, you found him interesting.

LOLA   I love you, Ben, and that love is not contingent on whether your knuckles are rough or—

BEN   I'm not so different from him in many ways, you know, I could do all the same things, given different—

LOLA   Why are you afraid to touch me?

> *Elsewhere: CLAIRE goes to her window. She looks out at MARSHALL's house, his windowsill (the window having been shattered); he's not there. Her face falls. She grabs her flashlight, turns it on and off a couple times in quick succession, to catch his attention should he be there to see it. Nothing happens. But then, snapping her flashlight on again, she notices something: a sign, pieces of paper taped together, is hung across the sill. "I'M SORRY," it says. "PLEASE COME BACK."*
>
> *LEON, across the street, is in shadow. Silence.*

BEN   He's back.

> *BEN, CLAIRE and LOLA, in their house.*

LOLA   He's what?

BEN   He's out there right now. Leon. He's parked across the street.

CLAIRE   Oh shit.

LOLA   Nice mouth, Claire. Why would he come back—?

BEN   I'm gonna do something.

LOLA   Just call the police, Ben.

BEN   No.

CLAIRE   Just call the police, Dad.

BEN   It's fine. It'll be fine.

LOLA   What are you going to do?

BEN   Let me take care of it.

LOLA   Ben—

BEN   This is an exceptional situation.

LOLA   I know that, but—

BEN   You know I don't believe that violence is a means to anything.

Swiftly off he goes.

LOLA   But why would he come back?

They're alone now, LOLA, CLAIRE and MARSHALL, alone together. There is a sense of ritual preparation, a sense of hush. MARSHALL comes to his window, watches.

CLAIRE   I see him right away.

LOLA   I see him too.

MARSHALL   I see him too.

CLAIRE   I watch my father go and I'm choking, I'm gasping, I can't catch my breath, and I'm afraid for Leon, I want to protect him, but why the fuck should I care about *him*—?

LOLA   I want my husband to come home with blood on his hands.

MARSHALL   I lose sight of them so quickly—

CLAIRE   Because he's like me, because I'm like him, that must be it, because I'm broken like him, wrong like him—will somebody fix me, please—?

LOLA   I want him to come home with blood on his hands and to take his hands and to place them on my face.

MARSHALL   I lose sight of them so, so quickly—

CLAIRE   I'd give anything for someone to fix me and make me normal, you know, like a *normal* person, who wants *normal* things, and has a boyfriend, and has friend friends, and doesn't break people's windows, often, and falls in love at the age of fourteen and gets married and has lots of kids and a nicer cleaner house than her mother's—you know *normal*—is that possible? Can anybody make that possible for me, please—?

LOLA   And tell me I exist.

CLAIRE   What a cruel, stupid joke! Why was I made able to love like fucking crazy but unable to earn love from anyone else—?

LOLA   Not with words. With his hands on my face.

MARSHALL   I lose sight of them so, so quickly, and then I know nothing, because that's the limit, isn't it, what you can see of people, that's all you get, and that's dangerous, that kind of ignorance, too dangerous for me, thanks, from now on I'm keeping my binoculars trained on the sky, because you don't get hurt that way, because that way you don't find yourself waking up in the middle of the night unable to catch your breath, and you're fine, and you're okay, and you've got everything you need, by yourself, in your house, in your room, in your little darkened corner—from now on, from now on—

LOLA   And we'll bathe together and watch the blood wash off.

MARSHALL   I'll close my eyes. I'll watch the inside of my head. Why shouldn't that be enough?

CLAIRE   Can you give me a reason, one reason, one fucking little teensy tiny reason, why I shouldn't find another speeding car and cross the street?

BEN   I follow him across the city. To his home. To the place where he sleeps.

> *Sound of rapping at a door. Rapping harder, with more urgency, with more violence. Sound of a door opening. Light on BEN and LEON.*

LEON   ...you.

> *Black. Light rises on the faces of CLAIRE, LOLA and MARSHALL. Watching. Listening.*
>
> *Sounds of an apartment being torn to pieces: wood snapped, the legs kicked out from under a kitchen table; a toaster flung against tile; doors ripped off cupboards, food poured out of cans and boxes; pages and pages torn from books. And only a single human voice:*

...stop... please... please stop...

> *But he's in darkness. Only the faces of CLAIRE, LOLA and MARSHALL. Watching. Listening.*
>
> *Sound of plates breaking, cutlery clattering onto tile. Sound of a knife slashing up a mattress, a pillow. Sound of a television smashed. And only a single human voice:*

...no...no no no, Ben, no, no, no, no...

> *But darkness yet. Only the faces of CLAIRE, LOLA and MARSHALL. Watching. Listening.*
>
> *Sound of glass breaking.*
>
> *Crescendo.*
>
> *Light on BEN and LEON, in LEON's apartment.*
>
> *BEN hits LEON in the face, breaking his nose. LEON falls. BEN kicks him. He kicks him again. He kicks him clear off the ground. LEON does not fight back. It goes on.*
>
> *BEN stops.*

Silence.

BEN stands above LEON, fixed to the spot. LEON is weeping. BEN is watching LEON weep. BEN's out of breath. He's shaking.

...God help me.

BEN   ...tell me what I should do.

LEON   ...God help me. Somebody help me.

BEN   ...tell me what I should do, tell me what's right, what would you do in my position?

BEN reaches out and takes LEON's hand. He squeezes LEON's hand, he wraps his fingers around LEON's fingers.

...I mean look at this. Look at this. I barely know you. I barely even know you.

He takes LEON's hand into both of his.

...I've got to go. I've got to go. I've got to get in my car and—

LEON   No.

BEN   ...

LEON   No, would you just...

BEN   ...

LEON   Just don't leave right this minute.

BEN   ...

LEON   Could you just... stay here... a little longer.

BEN   ...

LEON   And I'm not... I mean I don't want anything, nothing, I just... don't go.

BEN   ...

LEON   Don't go.

BEN   I won't.

LEON   Don't go.

BEN   I'm not going.

LEON   Just five minutes.

BEN   ...

LEON   Okay. Okay.

BEN   It's okay. It's gonna be okay.

LEON   Just five minutes. Just stay here with me for five minutes.

BEN   ...

LEON   Okay. Okay.

BEN   ...

LEON   ...

> *Long silence.*

> *LOLA comes forward. She places her hands on BEN's shoulders.*

LOLA   Are we safe?

> *LOLA takes LEON's place. LEON is gone. The bedroom.*

BEN   ...I'd like you to tell me what you need from me.

LOLA   What do you mean?

BEN   What I said. Tell me what you need from me. I love you. I don't want to lose you.

LOLA   I never suggested—

> *He kisses her.*

...I need you to look at me. I need you to look at me and not look away.

BEN   And?

LOLA   No "and."

BEN   I can do that.

LOLA   ...and what do you need from me.

BEN   ...tell me I'm a good man.

LOLA   ...

BEN   Or good enough.

> *She kisses him passionately. He kisses her back.*

MARSHALL   What can you see?

> *BEN and LOLA are gone.*

CLAIRE   Nothing.

MARSHALL   Nothing?

CLAIRE   No lights on in the house.

MARSHALL   Does that mean we're alone?

> *They're in his bedroom. It's before dawn. CLAIRE looks through the binoculars. He looks at her. She lowers the binoculars. He moves ever so tentatively to touch her face.*

CLAIRE   ...I'm afraid of you.

MARSHALL   I don't think I'm going to hurt you.

CLAIRE   You don't think?

MARSHALL   No. Not on purpose.

> *A moment. He walks to the windowsill.*

Come here.

CLAIRE   ...

MARSHALL   I want you to see the sunrise break over the top of your chimney.

> *Slowly she goes to him. They look.*

CLAIRE   How long.

MARSHALL   Moments.

> *A beat. Another.*

> *The sun rises. Morning light finds their faces.*

So.

CLAIRE   ...

MARSHALL   Do you feel alive?

CLAIRE   ...I don't know how to answer that.

> *He raises the binoculars to his eyes. Looks off, out.*

Marshall.

MARSHALL   Yes?

CLAIRE   What are you looking at?

MARSHALL   ...

CLAIRE   Look at me.

> *A moment. Slowly, his binoculars pressed to his eyes, he turns to her.*

...can you see me?

He adjusts the focus on the binoculars. The zoom. They are two feet apart.

...am I there?

He takes a step closer to her.

MARSHALL   My God.

CLAIRE   What is it?

MARSHALL   ...you're everywhere.

He steps closer to her. Almost touching her. The other end of the binoculars meets her face. The lenses press up against her eyes. His eyes and hers are connected. They stand like this together for a moment. Then, holding the binoculars in place, as one, they move their lips towards each other. Straining. They press and press. But their mouths won't reach. They are an unbridgeable inch apart.

CLAIRE   ...it's difficult.

But they keep trying.

The end.

The Russian Play

by Hannah Moscovitch

Hannah Moscovitch is a 2001 graduate of the National Theatre School's acting program, and in that same year she founded Absit Omen Theatre with her classmate, Michael Rubenfeld. Hannah began focusing on playwriting in 2002, when her play *Cigarettes and Tricia Truman* was staged as part of the Great Canadian Theatre Company's FourPlay Series.

Hannah's other plays include *Essay*, which premiered at SummerWorks Festival in 2005, where it won the Contra Guys Award for Best New Play. *The Russian Play* also premiered that year at SummerWorks, where it was awarded the Jury Prize for Best New Production. Both plays were remounted as part of a double bill at Factory Theatre in winter 2008. *East of Berlin*, written while Hannah was part of the Tarragon Playwrights Unit, premiered at that theatre in the fall of 2007.

A native of Ottawa, Hannah now lives in Toronto, where she is playwright-in-residence at Tarragon Theatre. She has been commissioned to create new works for the stage with a number of Canada's most exciting established and experimental theatre companies, including Prairie Theatre Exchange in Winnipeg, Volcano Theatre in Toronto, and 2b theatre company in Halifax. Hannah is a member of the Playwrights Guild of Canada.

"Love is a dangerous joy."
—Federico García Lorca

The Russian Play was originally produced in August, 2006 by Company Theatre Crisis and Absit Omen Theatre, as part of the SummerWorks Theatre Festival, Toronto, with the following company:

SONYA	Michelle Monteith
PIOTR	Aaron Willis
KOSTYA	Shawn Campbell
VIOLINIST	Tom Howell

Directed by Natasha Mytnowych
Set and costume design byCamellia Koo and Natasha Mytnowych
Original music composed by Claire Jenkins with Tom Howell
Stage managed by Julia Lederer

The Russian Play won the 2006 SummerWorks Jury Prize for Outstanding New Production.

The Russian Play was later produced at Factory Theatre in Toronto as part of a double bill with *Essay* in January of 2008, with the following company:

SONYA	Michelle Monteith
PIOTR	Aaron Willis
KOSTYA	Shawn Campbell
VIOLINIST	Tom Howell

Directed by Natasha Mytnowych
Musical direction by Claire Jenkins
Asstistant directed by Julia Lederer
Choreographed by Monica Dottor
Set & costume designed by Camellia Koo
Lighting designed by Kimberly Purtell
Original music composed by Claire Jenkins with Tom Howell
Asstistant Set & costume design by Anna Treusch
Stage managed by Joanna Barrotta
Asstistant stage managed by Alexandra Stephanoff

Characters

SONYA, the flower-shop girl: various ages, starting at sixteen
PIOTR, the gravedigger: twenties
KOSTYA, the Kulak's son: thirties

THE RUSSIAN PLAY

The characters speak with Russian accents.

The VIOLINIST plays The Russian Play refrain in the darkness. Lights come up on SONYA. She is dressed in a ragged skirt and a shawl. She holds a piece of bread. She picks a hair off of it.

SONYA   Is a little wet. But is okay. I wish for some vodka to offer to you, but only this bread.

SONYA contemplates the audience.

Ahn! I see what you are thinking. You are thinking this is Russian play, you are thinking Chekhov, Tolstoy, so boring. And Russia. Shitty country. Stalin, Kremlin, KGB. And as you are thinking this, you are looking in program to see if there is intermission when you can leave.

Beat.

No intermission! But, please, let me reassure to you that I am wanting for your amusement, and also your illumination on many subjects. But mostly on subject of love.

Beat.

Ahn! Now I have got for myself your attention. Okay, so, I am wanting to answer for all of you important question. Very important question is… where do you hide piece of bread? Ahn? Where do you hide? In the shoe? Yes? In the shoe?

Beat.

First place they look.

SONYA holds out the bread.

Where do you hide piece of bread? I ask myself this, I am looking for answer, and as I am looking for answer, I am thinking of girl. She is mistress of gravedigger in small Russian town, Vladekstov.

The lights flicker. When the lights come up, the bread is gone out of her hands.

Ahn yes, the shit lights. I am sorry to apologize.

Beat.

Okay, so, I am thinking of mistress of gravedigger. She is working in flower shop. Beautiful flower shop very close to graveyard. On way to graveyard, many people are thinking, "I would like some flowers," and there is shop, very good for business. Also good for business, girl in shop with nice figure, saying always, "What can I get for you, Mister?"

Beat.

Her name is Sonya. And the gravedigger, Piotr. Always the shop owner is saying, "Go Sonya, take these flowers to the church for funeral." And Sonya, she is walking by graveyard, and there is Piotr.

Lights come up on PIOTR in a graveyard, digging a grave. SONYA curtseys to him and he nods at her.

(to audience) And Piotr is saying to her.

PIOTR   Hello, Sonya.

SONYA   *(to audience)* And Sonya is saying. *(to PIOTR)* Hello Piotr.

SONYA watches PIOTR dig the grave.

Has someone died?

PIOTR   Yes. Dasha, the baker's second daughter.

SONYA   Oh no, but she was so young and so beautiful!

PIOTR   Yes, but not so beautiful as you, Sonya.

Lights out on PIOTR.

SONYA   *(to the audience)* So you see how it was between them.

Beat.

Sometime, the shop owner say to Sonya, "Look at these flowers for wedding of Kulak's son. He is marrying that no-good girl, Anya. Always wearing fur, how can she afford? But is his funeral, if he want to marry flashy girl who will spend all his money, then he can have pricy flowers for cheap wife." And Sonya would say, "Don't trouble yourself for taking the flowers. I will take them over to the Kulak's house if you don't like." And Sonya would take the flowers on a long walk all the way to the churchyard where Piotr is digging.

Lights up on PIOTR in a graveyard. She curtseys and he nods.

PIOTR   Hello Sonya.

SONYA   Hello Piotr.

SONYA watches him dig the grave.

Has someone died?

PIOTR   Yes. And if you come a little closer, I will show to you.

PIOTR beckons to her. She looks in both directions and hesitates. He holds out his hand.

Come!

SONYA approaches. He shows her the grave. She hesitates.

Look.

SONYA peers over the edge. She can't see very well, so she leans in.

Don't fall in, Sonya!

He grabs and holds her. She laughs and disentangles herself.

SONYA   Piotr! There's no one down here!

PIOTR   Not yet, no, but soon. Winter is coming. So cold in Vladekstov. So cold, and what to do to warm up?

PIOTR leans in to kiss SONYA. As their lips touch, the lights go out on PIOTR.

SONYA   *(to audience)* So you see how it was between them.

Beat.

There is song Piotr is always singing, in Russian, but I translate for you. Okay, ahn, song goes....

SONYA speaks the song, translating.

Laughing, laughing, over the fields,
Over the fields, ha ha ha, we go laughing
Until the snow comes
Freezing the river and the sky and the birds
And my love for you.

SONYA contemplates the audience.

Is better in Russian.

SONYA sings a little of the song in Russian.

Smee-yom-sya, smee-yom-sya, cheerez pol-ya,
Cheerez pol-ya, ha ha ha, mi smee-yom-sya.

SONYA cuts herself off.

Okay, but think of Piotr singing.

SONYA sings a few more words of the song. PIOTR enters and sings with her.

SONYA/PIOTR   *A kakda Prid-yot sneg*

Zam yorz-nit ree-ka, eh nebo, eh pzee-zi
Eh mo-you lyou-bov teeb-yeh.

SONYA   Where did you learn this song, Piotr?

PIOTR   In Moscow.

SONYA   Moscow! When were you in Moscow?

PIOTR   Right after I was in Leningrad.

SONYA   Leningrad!

PIOTR   And now I am in Vladekstov, making new life for myself in new Russia.

> *PIOTR smiles at SONYA, holds her.*

There is `nother part of the song, Sonya, and is best part, but you don't sing.

SONYA   What other part, Piotr?

PIOTR   Ahn! Let me sing to you!

> *PIOTR sings to her.*

You are just a little piece of Russia,
Sonya, just a little piece,
But you are the most beautiful piece of Russia,
Sonya, the most beautiful piece.

> *PIOTR sings the song and they dance. Lights out on PIOTR.*

SONYA   *(to audience)* You see? You fall in love with him too!

> *Beat.*

One day, Sonya is singing in flower shop this song of Piotr's. The shop owner, she laugh when she hear and she say, "That is gravedigger's song! Is good song for him." Sonya say, "Yes, because he digs graves is right he sing sad song of love." But the shop owner, she look around kind of sneaky and then she whisper to Sonya, "Or maybe his wife taught it to him. She gives him so much troubles, he'd rather dig graves in Vladekstov than live with her in Moscow." And she laugh at this very funny joke.

> *Beat.*

Ha ha ha.

> *Beat.*

Okay, so, heart of Sonya is broken. But heart is very strong organ. You can rip it out and put it back in again and it still work okay. So what is big problem? Why is Sonya waiting for Piotr to come by with his shovel? Why go and wait in the cold? Why not forget about him?

Beat.

Because... in less than nine months she will have something to remember him by.

Lights up on PIOTR in the graveyard.

PIOTR   Sonya? Why are you standing here? You look so cold!

SONYA   Yes, I am cold, Piotr. I am cold, but your wife in Moscow is colder!

As PIOTR is about to justify himself, the lights go out on him.

This is shit part of love.

Beat.

Sonya is stupid girl, yes? She like his stupid song, and she get into bed with him, and now she's this problem. Very stupid. But, when woman is sixteen, she is like.... No, I forget it. Ahn! When she is forty, she is like Europe, because she is in ruins, like America when she is twenty-five, at height of powers, when she is sixteen like Africa, undiscovered country.

Beat.

Undiscovered and stupid Sonya.

Beat.

Ahn yes, and Russia! When woman is sixty, she is like Russia. Every-one knows where it is, but no one wants to go there.

Beat.

Ladies, you can't see, but all the men are nodding.

Beat.

Now Sonya is walking back to flower shop in the cold, she is lying in the cold bed, listening to the cold outside, thinking about Piotr's words. He is saying to her, "Don't worry, Sonya. I won't leave you like this, I will help with problem. Come back tomorrow at the end of the day when Vladekstov is sleeping."

Beat.

All day Sonya is wrapping flowers and wrapping flowers. The shop owner say to her, "What Sonya, you are not singing? Don't like that song so much anymore?" And she laugh to herself.

Beat.

Ha ha ha.

Beat.

When the flower shop is quiet, and the shop owner is sleeping, Sonya put back on her clothes, put back on her shoes, wrap her shawl around her, and walk to graveyard where Piotr is waiting.

> *Lights up on PIOTR in the graveyard. He holds his shovel and a small sack of tools. He beckons to her.*

PIOTR   Come, Sonya. Lie down.

> *SONYA doesn't move.*

(*gently*) Come.

> *SONYA doesn't move. PIOTR reaches down and touches the earth.*

Don't worry, it's not so cold.

Beat.

Please, Sonya, I— I worked in hospital in Moscow—

> *SONYA turns to leave but lingers.*

Beat.

I know I'm not a good person, Sonya, but I love you, and I won't hurt you.

Beat.

(*gentle*) Come.

> *SONYA and PIOTR hold their pose. The VIOLINIST walks across the stage, playing sweetly at first, then making discordant, jarring sounds as he passes between the lovers. Time elapses. PIOTR is digging a small grave in the moonlight. We hear the sound of his shovel hitting the stage. SONYA is holding her shawl wrapped into the shape of a baby.*

SONYA   Why so big a grave, Piotr?

> *Beat.*

Doesn't need to be so big.

Beat.

Just little.

Beat.

Just a little piece of blanket.

> *PIOTR stops digging, crosses himself and walks away. SONYA stands over the grave and holds the baby over it. As she lets the baby fall, it transforms back into her shawl.*

(to the audience) Okay, so problem of Sonya is…!

> *SONYA contemplates the audience.*

Ahn, yes, I see what you are thinking. You are thinking, here comes Russian part of the play. Well, is Russian play. Some laughing, and then misery!

> *Beat.*

(trying to cheer up the audience) Okay, so, is okay. Don't worry, problem of Sonya is solved. Maybe she's a little uncomfortable in the heart, and also between the legs, but love is shit like that, ahn ladies?

> *Beat.*

On walk home to flower shop, Sonya is feeling little better. She is thinking, next time she fall in love with Kulak's son, running lots of factory, not with gravedigger with wife in Moscow.

> *Beat.*

When Sonya go into flower shop, she take off her shoes and walk on tip of toes for not to make any noise. She get to little corner in back of shop where she sleep. She take off shawl and she take off skirt, and there is shop owner standing in doorway.

> *Beat.*

Shop owner with look on face like she drink bad vodka and want to spit it out.

> *Beat.*

Sonya say to her, "Hello, I'm sorry, I went for walk in cold to feel better. I was sick." Shop owner nod her head and smile, but not so nice a smile, and she say, "Ahn sick, that's what you call it? Did he make you feel better? That Moscow gravedigger? He digs graves all over Russia, I hear."

> *Beat.*

"No, I told you I was sick!" But the shop owner say, "Where did you lie down with him, in the graveyard? Whose grave did you lie on? That little boy Dmitri, died of fever? Or Varya, good wife to butcher for twenty-three years?"

Beat.

"No, is not true!" But the shop owner say to Sonya, "You smell like corpse. Can't have that smell in my shop. Make the flowers die. Make the customers sick to their stomach." And she push Sonya out of the door.

Beat.

Winter is not so good a time to look for job, and in Vladekstov, gossip is like drinking vodka. How else to make the time go by? Soon, whole town know about the flower-shop girl and the gravedigger. The men are saying, "That Sonya. I wouldn't mind being gravedigger if such girls come to you." And the wives are saying, "Anh yes, that Sonya, I always say she was trouble."

Beat.

Piotr? He leave back to his wife in Moscow on first train out of Vladekstov. And Sonya? She is shit out for work. Who will give job to no-good ex-mistress of gravedigger?

Beat.

She ask at factory, she ask at farm, but....

Beat.

Soon, Sonya leave Vladekstov and travel to nearby Smolensk. But even in Smolensk, with lots of shop, lots of factory, work is not so easy to find.

Beat.

Soon, Sonya's skirt is a little dirty, her hair is a little greasy, the skin fall away from the bone.

Beat.

Soon, she is selling flowers in the streets. In the streets, she is selling flowers....

Beat.

We all know what happens to flower-shop girls when they run out of rubles, yes? They learn that love have...

KOSTYA enters.

...market value.

(to KOSTYA) Mister, please, some flowers for you? Some flowers, mister?

KOSTYA   I remember you. *(He considers her.)* From Vladekstov! From the shop, by the graveyard, yes?

SONYA   Yes.

KOSTYA   *(trying to remember her name)* Sonya?

SONYA   Yes.

KOSTYA   Yes, that's right. Sonya, in the flowershop. So young and so beautiful.

SONYA   You are Kostya, the Kulak's son.

KOSTYA   That's right.

SONYA   Married to that no-good girl, Anya.

> *SONYA laughs, then puts her head down, embarrassed.*

KOSTYA   That's funny.

SONYA   I brought flowers to your house for the wedding.

KOSTYA   Tell me, Sonya. I hear you like graveyards. Do you also like factories?

> *SONYA pulls away.*

No, please, I'm sorry. Look, let me buy some flowers. They're very beautiful. Very beautiful flowers for sale.

> *Lights out on KOSTYA.*

SONYA   *(to audience)* Here is rich Kúlak's son in Smolensk! Buying flowers from Sonya in Smolensk, can you believe? Can you believe such luck of this?!

> *Beat.*

He have wife, yes, he have wife, but who don't have wife, ahn, ladies?

> *SONYA sings the Russian song, flirting with KOSTYA. SONYA begins to sing and dance for him.*

Smee-yom-sya, smee-yom-sya,
Cheerez pol-ya,
Cheerez pol-ya, ha ha ha,
Mee smee-yom-sya.

KOSTYA   I like this song.

> *SONYA sits on KOSTYA's lap.*

SONYA   *(flirting)* Tell me. Are all men cold in their wives' beds?

KOSTYA *(laughs)* Yes. You still think of him? Your Moscow gravedigger.

SONYA No.

KOSTYA No?

SONYA No gravedigger, please, big mistake. What can he do for you? Ahn? What? Maybe dig grave for you when you are dead?!

> *KOSTYA laughs.*

Did you bring me here to laugh at me?

KOSTYA No.

SONYA No, I didn't think so.

> *They kiss. As they kiss, the lights fade out on KOSTYA.*

(to audience) Okay! So! We all understand the picture here.

> *Beat.*

The Kulak's son, he keep Sonya in little room in hotel. He come to see her twice, three times, sometime four times a week. Soon people of Smolensk hear about the Kulak's son and the ex-flower-shop girl. But this time, no one say anything. Because the Kulak's son? He is not just in bed with Sonya. He is also in bed with secret police, with Soviet bureaucrat. And who knows, maybe with Stalin himself.

> *Lights up on KOSTYA, in the hotel room.*

KOSTYA I like this Stalin. Either you want new Russia, or you don't want new Russia. And Stalin? He want new Russia.

SONYA Just like you, Kostya.

> *KOSTYA kisses her hand.*

KOSTYA Sonya, Sonya! My little shop girl.

SONYA Kostya. Please.

KOSTYA There are lots of girls like you, Sonya, factories full of them. But I don't know why— why I…!

> *Beat.*

I could pick any girl. But—

SONYA You will be late for your wife, Kostya. She will be angry.

KOSTYA I don't care! I don't care about my wife!

SONYA You will care when she's yelling at you!

KOSTYA   No I won't, I won't listen, I will think of you in this little room, looking like flower!

> *SONYA and KOSTYA laugh, and he spins her around and admires her. The lights fade on him as he exits. SONYA stops laughing and contemplates the audience.*

SONYA   *(to audience)* Not so simple what to think of this Kulak's son. Some of you are thinking Kostya is good enough man, lots of factories, lots of rubles. Sonya is okay, is looked after. So why are you still sitting here? Why is play still going?

> *Beat.*

But some of you are having more romantic thought. Ahn? Ladies!?

> *Beat.*

Sonya try not to think about Piotr. She try not to think about Piotr when Kostya come to see her, when Kostya look at her, when he put his arms around her.

> *PIOTR enters as SONYA says the above. He puts his arms around her, holds her, kisses her. SONYA smiles. The lights flicker. Now it's KOSTYA holding her.*

KOSTYA   *(sexual)* Sonya, Sonya!

SONYA   Kostya, Kostya, will you—

KOSTYA   *(sexual)* What?

SONYA   —bring me... glass of vodka?

> *KOSTYA stops short, looks at her, exits.*

(to audience) For long time, Sonya live in hotel in Smolensk, she keep her mouth shut, and she hold down misery. She hold down misery using lots of vodka. But problem with vodka? It make you forget, but it also give you courage.

> *Lights up on KOSTYA.*

KOSTYA   I am meeting with police. They are waiting for me, Sonya, I can't fight with you right now.

SONYA   So don't fight with me.

KOSTYA   Come Sonya, please, don't be crazy. My wife is crazy, I don't need more crazy, okay?

> *Beat.*

(indulging her) Where would you go?

SONYA   I don't know. Moscow?

KOSTYA   Moscow. I don't understand. Why don't you love me? What? You love gravedigger but you don't love me? Why not?

> *Beat.*

Why not?

SONYA   Look after your wife!

KOSTYA   No, tell me, why don't you love me, Sonya?

SONYA   I don't know! I try, but—

KOSTYA   Who are you not to love me? Flower-shop girl with bad history. Opening your legs to gravediggers and Soviet traitors.

SONYA   That's right, I'm just ex-flower-shop girl with shit luck and bad history, so why not let me go? Lots of other girls!

> *KOSTYA holds SONYA. She struggles.*

KOSTYA   Please, Sonya, I love you, don't be crazy.

> *SONYA hits him and pushes him away. KOSTYA stumbles. He steadies himself. KOSTYA looks at her, considers, seems to make a decision, exits.*

SONYA   *(to audience)* What can I tell to you? Sonya is stupid girl, yes? Stupid Russian girl, lots of girls like Sonya, factories full of them.

> *Beat.*

So. Vodka is not so strong now, and Sonya is not so sure anymore what her big idea was when she wanted to go to Moscow. But, as Kostya leave her hotel room, as she think about long train to Moscow, she feel like light is shining on her. She pack her bag, she put on her shawl, she open the door and there is police standing in doorway.

> *Beat.*

Police with look on their faces like they eat bad pork and want to spit it out.

> *Beat.*

"Hello," Sonya say to police, "I am just leaving for Moscow. Did Kostya send you for something?" The police nod their heads, and they smile to each other, and they say to her, "You want to go to Moscow, Sonya? Is no problem, let us take you. Is maybe not so comfortable in Moscow as here in Smolensk, but don't worry, we will look after you."

> *Beat.*

"No, is okay," Sonya say to the police, "I don't want you to take me. Tell Kostya I don't want to go anymore. Tell him I want to stay in Smolensk." The police laugh when they hear this, and they say, "What? You don't like Moscow so much anymore? Well then, what about Siberia?"

> *Beat.*

"No, wait. Please, Kostya is not happy with me now, but, if you let me speak with him, he will change back his mind. Please, please let me speak to him. Let me speak to him!"

> *Beat.*

Sonya travel to Moscow in cattlecart of train.

> *Beat.*

Sonya travel for three days, alone with police, in cattlecart of train.

> *We hear PIOTR, off, singing the Russian song.*

In Moscow prison, Sonya start to go a little crazy.

> *Beat.*

Maybe is because of the police interrogations. Maybe is because they tell her to say she is enemy of people so they can send her to work camp, maybe because they don't give for her anything to eat, because they pull out her fingernails one by one and leave her standing in cold water for many hours, maybe because she is turning into just blood and bones, sometime Sonya think she can hear Piotr singing.

> *SONYA listens to the singing.*

Singing like he used to sing to her in Vladekstov graveyard.

> *Beat.*

(*calling*) Piotr?

> *The singing and the violin cut out. SONYA listens for a moment and then looks away. After a moment, the singing starts again.*

Sonya is going a little crazy.

> *Beat.*

> *PIOTR steps into the light.*

PIOTR   Sonya?

SONYA   Piotr?

PIOTR   Sonya.

SONYA Piotr. You are police now?

PIOTR No. I am working in graveyard, back of prison.

> *PIOTR stares at her. SONYA tries to straighten her skirt.*

SONYA I not looking like you remember?

PIOTR No, Sonya you look.... You need bread, I think I have.

> *PIOTR reaches into his pocket.*

SONYA How is wife? She is here in Moscow, yes?

PIOTR No.

SONYA No?

PIOTR No. She... died. Not long after I left Vladekstov.

> *Beat.*

SONYA Wife died?

PIOTR Yes.

SONYA And you didn't come back? You didn't come back to Vladekstov and look for me? Why not? Why didn't you come. Why wouldn't you come back, Piotr?

PIOTR Because! Because of Kulak. Kulak in Smolensk, yes? You were happy? You were looked after?

SONYA No!

PIOTR You were not happy?

SONYA No! How could I be happy? I loved you! I loved you, Piotr.

PIOTR Sonya, I loved you too. I loved you and I left you there. I left you and life was difficult and full of misery, and I loved you, I don't know why I—

> *PIOTR reacts to footsteps he hears, off. He steps back and looks down the corridor.*

SONYA Is police coming?

> *Beat.*

Piotr? Is police?

> *PIOTR steps toward her.*

PIOTR *(low)* Sonya, take bread. Don't show.

PIOTR hands her the bread, looks behind him and then quickly turns away and exits.

SONYA   *(calling after him)* Is police? Piotr!

> *Beat.*

(to audience) Sonya is thinking, the bread! The bread Piotr give to her! The police will see and will want to know where is from, and what will she say? Not from Piotr. She can't say from Piotr, or they will....

> *Beat.*

Sonya know what will happen to Piotr if she tell them that he....

> *Beat.*

She have to hide the bread, so they can't find, the police who look everywhere. Is big piece, where to hide? She stuff into mouth but is too big. She can't put in shoe, they look in shoe, she can't put in skirt, they look in skirt. Can't put in stocking, they look in stocking. Where to hide piece of bread, I ask myself this. I am looking for answer.

> *SONYA reaches between her skirts and all the way up, and with a little jerk, she pulls out a piece of bread. She holds it out. She picks a hair off of it.*

Stupid place to put bread.

> *Beat.*

Stupid Sonya.

> *Beat.*

Doesn't think of infection.

> *Beat.*

Infection from bread, can you believe?

> *Beat.*

For two weeks Sonya is in prison hospital ward, slowing turning black.

> *PIOTR starts digging her grave, off. SONYA crumbles the bread in her hand. She contemplates the audience.*

Okay. So. Let me level to you. This is my shit Russian love story. Stupid, stupid Sonya, I am embarrass to myself. I fall in love with Piotr, and that's my whole life gone for shit.

> *PIOTR continues digging, off.*

I lose flower-shop job for Piotr, Kostya send police for me for Piotr, and now, in Moscow prison, I kill myself for Piotr. This is love for you!

Beat.

Ladies, I have to tell you, you won't like to hear, but love is like Russia. There are some beautiful pieces, but mostly it's shit. Ahn, ladies? You were thinking is beautiful, my story? The gravedigger and the flower-shop girl, is like poetry, yes?

Beat.

Well! Let me tell to you. Love is—!

PIOTR enters and puts his arms around SONYA. She feels his warmth. She is terribly, terribly happy.

The VIOLINIST stops playing abruptly. SONYA is dead in PIOTR's arms. As PIOTR lays SONYA in the grave, the lights fade out.

Spain

by Michael Rubenfeld

Michael Rubenfeld is a writer, actor, director and producer. He is the author of *Present Tense*, which premiered at the 2003 SummerWorks Festival, and was subsequently presented in Lenox, Massachusetts as part of Shakespeare and Co.'s New Work Festival, and in Ensemble Studio Theatre's Octoberfest in New York City. In 2004 Michael wrote, directed and produced *Spain* as part of the 2004 SummerWorks Festival, where it was named Outstanding New Play/Production by *NOW* Magazine. *Spain* went on to have a second production in October 2006 in the Tarragon Theatre Extra Space.

In May 2008, Michael directed his new play, *My Fellow Creatures*, at Theatre Passe Muraille, as an Absit Omen Theatre/Buddies in Bad Times co-production.

Originally from Winnipeg, Michael graduated in 2001 from the National Theatre School's acting program. He now lives in Toronto where, in 2008, he was appointed Artistic Producer of the SummerWorks Theatre Festival. Michael is also the co-founder and co-artistic director of Absit Omen Theatre, along with Hannah Moscovitch.

To the love I have, the love I had and the love I lost.

Spain was first produced in August 2004 as part of the SummerWorks
Theatre Festival at Theatre Passe Muraille Backspace, Toronto, with the
following company:

ERIC   Gray Powell
JARED   Aaron Willis
BETH   Kimwun Perehinec

Directed by Michael Rubenfeld
Assistant Direction by Caleb Yong
Lighting Design by André Du Toit
Stage Managed by Kathryn Westoll
Music by Matthew MacFadzean
Fight Direction by Todd Campbell
Poster Design by Stéphane Monnet
Photography by Joey Morin

Spain was also produced in October 2006 by diy theatre/Kneeling Bus
Theatre/Absit Omen Theatre at the Tarragon Theatre Extra Space with the
following company:

ERIC   Steve Puchalski
JARED   Justin Conley
BETH   Siobhan Power

Directed by Michael Rubenfeld
Set and Lighting Design by Jeff Logue
Stage Managed by Joanna Barotta
Fight Coaching by Richard Lee
Sound Design by Dan Lee

Spain was developed and produced by Absit Omen Theatre (Toronto).

Characters

ERIC
JARED
BETH

Notes on Punctuation and Grammar

A "/" indicates that the next line should come in at that point in the previous line, having both characters speaking at once for a moment.

A "Beat." is a short pause, usually indicating a quick shift in thought.

A "Pause." is a longer pause, usually indicating a shift in tone, or a character needing more time to shift or to process thought.

Additional beats and pauses should not be used in the performance of the play unless found absolutely necessary. Some may be eliminated if desired.

Acknowledgements

This play would not have been possible without the wisdom and guidance of the following people: Claire Jenkins, Hannah Moscovitch, Peter Smith, Sarah Stanley, Matthew MacFadzean, Don Hannah, Tova Smith, Elana McMurtry and the Absitomeners.

SPAIN

Scene One – Jared's

> *ERIC and JARED sit in JARED's home. They've been drinking.*
> *They are sitting close.*

ERIC   I have to go.

> *Beat.*

Jared?

JARED   Go. If you have to go, then go.

> *Beat.*

I'm not stopping you.

ERIC   You're mad.

JARED   I'm not mad.

ERIC   I feel bad.

JARED   Why?

> *Beat.*

ERIC   You're allowed to feel mad.

JARED   Is that a patronizing tone?

ERIC   It isn't.

JARED   It sounds like a patronizing tone.

ERIC   I'm not patronizing you.

JARED   Because you know how much I love being patronized.

> *Pause.*

What do you want me to say Eric?

ERIC   Whatever you *need* to say.

> *Beat.*

Tell me what you're feeling.

JARED   I'm *feeling*? I'm feeling stupid.

ERIC   Why do you feel stupid?

JARED   Why are you using that tone?

ERIC   What tone?

JARED   That condescending tone.

ERIC   I'm not using a tone!

      Beat.

JARED   I don't know how I'm feeling. Okay?

ERIC   Okay.

      Beat.

JARED   I feel like crying.

ERIC   Really? Do you need to cry?

JARED   Is that what you want?

      Beat. A revelation.

That's what you want, isn't it.

ERIC   Maybe it'll make you—

JARED   No it / won't.

ERIC   Maybe it'll make you feel better.

JARED   Maybe it'll make *you* feel better?

ERIC   This isn't about / me.

JARED   How are *you* feeling?

ERIC   I'm not the one who…

JARED   Who what?

ERIC   Who's having a problem with—

JARED   What? Abandonment?

ERIC   I'm not abandon— I haven't abandoned you Jared. I'm incorporating Beth back into my life.

      Beat.

JARED   I liked it better when she was away and we could just talk about her.

      Beat.

ERIC   Are you serious?

JARED   Yes.

ERIC   That's retarded.

JARED   I know.

Beat.

I'm being a pussy.

ERIC   You're not being a pussy.

JARED   I'm a pussy.

ERIC   You're not—

JARED   I am. I'm a pussy.

ERIC   Fine. You're *my* pussy.

JARED   That's really great. I'm really, really pleased to be your pussy. You've already got a pussy.

ERIC   I can have two.

JARED   You don't need two.

ERIC   I do. I need two pussies.

JARED   Well you can't have two pussies!

Pause.

ERIC   Meow.

Beat.

It's good. You have some free time.

JARED   I don't want free time.

ERIC   You *need* free time.

JARED   No I don't.

ERIC   You need to work on the documentary.

JARED   It's stupid. I hate it and it's stupid.

ERIC   Why are you so angry?

JARED   I'm not angry, I'm...

Beat.

I missed my deadline for the rough edit.

Beat.

ERIC   I didn't know.

JARED   You didn't ask.

Beat.

ERIC How did you miss your deadline?

JARED I've been spending a lot of time with you.

ERIC Why didn't you tell me about the deadline?

> *Beat.*

When was it?

JARED Two weeks ago.

> *Beat.*

ERIC How could you miss / your deadline?

JARED It just happened. It's fine.

ERIC It's not fine—

JARED If we didn't spend as much time together—

ERIC Which is a problem we're solving.

JARED It's not a problem.

ERIC Clearly it is.

> *Beat.*

JARED Sometimes I feel like punching you in the face as hard as I can.

ERIC Sometimes I feel like punching YOU in the face—

JARED So punch me.

> *Beat.*

Punch me.

> *Pause.*

ERIC I love you.

JARED What?

ERIC Sorry.

> *Beat. A shift.*

She's been home a day.

JARED I know.

ERIC I need to…

JARED I know.

> *Beat.*

ERIC   I love her.

JARED   And that's no longer in question?

ERIC   It was never in question.

JARED   That's not true.

ERIC   I never questioned my _love_ for her.

JARED   What happened to the Eric who was really really afraid that when she gets back things will be different cry cry cry cry, and what if I don't love her when she gets back cry cry cry cry boo hoo Jared will you please wipe my ass for me because I CAN'T REACH.

>   _Beat._

So, that just went away?

>   _Beat._

ERIC   I should go.

JARED   Six months, Eric.

ERIC   It's complicated.

JARED   We've been talking about this for six months.

ERIC   You wouldn't understand.

JARED   Because I don't have a girlfriend?

ERIC   You don't have a relationship.

JARED   Relationships are scary.

ERIC   I know that. Do you? No. You don't.

JARED   Then why do you talk to me about your relationship?

ERIC   Fine. I'll stop.

JARED   No you won't.

ERIC   Fuck off.

JARED   I give it a day or two.

ERIC   For what?

JARED   Until you need me.

>   _Beat._

Shit.

>   _Beat._

ERIC   I gotta go.

JARED   I'm sorry.

ERIC   I'll see you later.

JARED   Can we hug?

ERIC   Why?

JARED   We always hug.

ERIC   No we don't.

JARED   *Always* hugging.

> *Beat. ERIC hugs JARED. Beat.*

ERIC   Okay?

JARED   Okay.

> *Beat.*

ERIC   Bye.

JARED   Bye.

> *Beat.*

ERIC   Sorry.

JARED   Why?

ERIC   I don't know.

> *Beat.*

JARED   Okay.

> *Beat.*

ERIC   Bye.

JARED   Bye.

> *Beat.*

ERIC   Bye.

JARED   Bye.

> *Beat.*

BOTH   Bye.

> *Blackout.*

Scene Two – Eric and Beth's Bedroom

In black, we hear the moans of a man. They are honest. Lights up on ERIC and BETH in bed. BETH is under the covers giving ERIC a blowjob. It's intense. ERIC lies topless in the bed, his hands over his head.

ERIC   It's so good.

> *BETH moans.*

Yeah.

> *ERIC reaches his hand down to BETH's head and strokes it lovingly. She comes up quickly from under the covers and kisses ERIC. She kisses his body. Devours it. She goes back down and continues.*

Jesus…

> *BETH comes back up quickly and kisses ERIC hard. She gets on top of him and starts fucking him. She's getting into it. Harder. ERIC tries to keep up, but he can't. He lies on his back, watching her, as she continues to fuck him. It becomes too much.*

Beth.

> *She doesn't respond. She continues. Working even harder.*

BETH.

> *Still nothing.*

BETH!

> *She stops. Surprised.*

BETH   What?

ERIC   What are you doing?

BETH   What do you think I'm doing?

ERIC   Take it easy.

BETH   Why?

ERIC   Go slow.

BETH   Go slow?

ERIC   Slow down.

BETH   Why?

ERIC   Just slow down.

> *Beat.*

BETH   Okay.

> *BETH, embarrassed, gets off him and lies on ERIC's chest. Pause.*

Sorry.

ERIC   Don't apologize.

> *And then… silence. A terrible, embarrassed, disappointed silence. ERIC puts his hand on her head and gently rubs it.*

Beth?

BETH   Mmm?

> *Beat.*

ERIC   We don't have to stop.

> *Beat.*

Beth?

> *Beat.*

We can keep going.

BETH   Sure.

> *Beat. ERIC gets on top of BETH. She's distant. He doesn't do anything.*

ERIC   Should I keep going?

BETH   Whatever you want.

> *Beat. ERIC starts to make love to BETH. She's still distant. He stops.*

ERIC   Do you want to keep / going.

BETH   We can stop if you want.

ERIC   Okay.

> *Beat.*

BETH   Sorry.

ERIC   No, I'm sorry.

> *ERIC gets off BETH. ERIC puts his head on BETH and holds her. It's awkward.*
>
> *Silence.*

Is that a new bra?

> *Beat.*

BETH I bought it today.

ERIC It's nice.

> *Beat.*

You look good.

BETH Thanks.

> *Beat.*

So do you.

> *Pause.*

There's a plate for you in the fridge.

ERIC I already ate.

BETH You did?

ERIC I had a slice on the way home.

BETH Way home from where?

ERIC Jared.

> *Beat.*

BETH You were with Jared?

ERIC Yeah.

> *Beat.*

BETH All night?

ERIC I guess.

> *Beat.*

BETH And how's Jared?

ERIC He's fine.

> *Beat. BETH stares at ERIC.*

What?

BETH Why didn't you come home?

ERIC I did come home. Look, I'm home.

BETH Why didn't you come home earlier?

ERIC Because, I was with Jared.

BETH You could have come home earlier. But you didn't. You stayed out with Jared.

ERIC Yeah?

BETH Just so we're clear: you could come home earlier, but you stayed out, drinking with Jared.

ERIC Yes.

BETH Which is why you can't fuck.

ERIC What?

BETH You can't fuck when you drink.

> *Beat.*

Sorry. That was mean.

ERIC No, you're right.

> *Beat.*

I should have come home.

BETH Why didn't you?

ERIC I needed a drink.

BETH So drink with *me*.

ERIC Okay. Next time I will.

BETH Good. Thank you.

ERIC You're welcome.

> *Beat.*

I looked for a job today.

BETH How did that go?

ERIC Not great. There's nothing shooting.

BETH Tell me about it.

> *Beat.*

ERIC Nice.

BETH Sorry. I'm sorry. *(She laughs.)* Sorry.

> *Beat.*

I've been gone six months.

ERIC I know.

BETH   I *worked* today.

ERIC   I know.

BETH   Today is my *second* day home.

ERIC   Yes, Beth.

BETH   My SECOND day, Eric. I got home YESTERDAY.

ERIC   I know.

BETH   I had to organize shifts from Italy.

ERIC   That was your choice.

BETH   Our hydro bill hasn't been paid in six months.

ERIC   I'll find work.

BETH   When?

ERIC   There's more work in the summer.

BETH   And until then?

>   *Beat.*

ERIC   I *had* a job. I got *fired* from my job. I'm a lousy grip.

BETH   You're a lazy grip.

ERIC   I hate gripping.

BETH   I hate coming home from the greatest trip of my life, and instead of painting, I'm selling pastels to born-again Christians needing to paint Jesus on the fucking cross for the *thirty-third* fucking time. And then I come home and I make a coconut curry because that's our favourite, but instead of eating with you, I'm eating, staring at the phone or the wall or the phone or the wall or the PHONE or the WALL while you're getting loaded with Jared.

>   *Beat.*

ERIC   You could have watched TV.

>   *Beat. BETH hits ERIC. ERIC hits her back. They play wrestle.*
>
>   *Pause.*

BETH   This isn't what I expected Eric.

ERIC   What did you expect?

BETH   I don't know.

ERIC   I'm sorry that I disappoint you.

BETH   Don't do that.

> *Beat.*

I just wished you'd have come home.

ERIC   I apologize. Okay? What else can I do?

> *Beat.*

BETH   You can make me feel special.

ERIC   You are. You are special

> *ERIC kisses BETH. He holds her head in his hands. At this moment, they are absolutely, one hundred percent, in love.*

You're special. I love you and you're special.

> *Beat.*

And I will work harder to make you feel special.

> *Beat.*

Okay?

> *Pause.*

BETH   I'm going to make some tea. *(beat)* Do you want some tea?

ERIC   I'll have some tea.

BETH   What kind of tea would you like?

ERIC   Whatever you're having.

BETH   Bengal Spice?

ERIC   Really?

BETH   You don't want Bengal Spice?

ERIC   No, it's fine.

BETH   What kind of tea would you like?

> *Beat.*

ERIC   Chamomile. With honey.

> *Beat. BETH goes to exit. ERIC hops up out of bed and stops her.*

(gently) Hey. Wait. Do you want me to make the tea?

> *Beat.*

BETH   Do you *want* to make the tea?

> *Beat.*

ERIC   I'll make the tea.

> *BETH exits.*

Scene Three – Jared's

JARED   And then?

ERIC   I made tea.

JARED   And after that?

ERIC   We drank the tea, we went to bed.

JARED   Did you fuck?

ERIC   No.

JARED   Did you cuddle?

ERIC   Not really.

> *Beat.*

Is that bad?

JARED   Not great. *(pause)* So what are you going to do?

ERIC   What *should* I do?

JARED   What do you think you should do?

ERIC   What do *you* think I should do?

JARED   What do *you think?*

ERIC   I don't know. *(beat)* What do you think?

> *Beat.*

What do you think?

JARED   I thought we weren't doing this anymore.

ERIC   Doing what?

> *Beat.*

JARED   Just so we're clear—you're talking to me about your relationship.

ERIC   What is that? "Just so we're clear." Beth says that—do I seem to be someone who's NOT CLEAR?

> *Beat. Yes. Yes he does.*

You're all I've got.

JARED   Bullshit.

ERIC   No it's / not!

JARED   You have a girlfriend.

ERIC   So?

JARED   You said—

ERIC   I need *you* right now.

> *Beat.*

I need you.

JARED   I know you need me. I told you that you'd *need me* you fucking twat.

> *Pause.*

You need to start using your head.

ERIC   How?

JARED   Use your head!

ERIC   How?!

JARED   Think!

ERIC   I don't know how!

JARED   Try harder!

ERIC   Don't talk down to me.

JARED   I'm not talking / down—

ERIC   Yes you are.

> *Beat.*

Sorry, I'm just feeling a little sensitive today.

> *Beat.*

JARED   You have a problem.

ERIC   I do. (*beat*) I do?

JARED   Beth. She's a problem.

ERIC   She is?

JARED   She sounds like a problem.

ERIC   Why?

JARED   She leaves for six months, comes home and immediately starts giving you ultimatums. That's a problem.

Beat.

Isn't that a problem?

ERIC   I guess so.

Beat.

Yeah, it's a problem.

Beat.

So what should I do?

JARED   Use your head!

ERIC   What does that MEAN!?

JARED   Make a decision! Do something.

ERIC   DO WHAT?

JARED   What do you want?

ERIC   I want to make things better.

JARED   How are you going to do that?

ERIC   I don't know Jared. I don't. Honestly, I feel…. Fuck!

Beat.

JARED   What's she doing today?

ERIC   Working.

JARED   Good. Buy her flowers, meet her at work, and eat her out.

Beat.

ERIC   Eat her out? At work?

JARED   Yes.

Beat.

ERIC   At work?

JARED   Yes.

Beat.

ERIC   That makes me uncomfortable.

Beat.

Do you *think* it'll work?

JARED   It could.

> *Beat.*

ERIC   So I what, I walk in and I just... what... I ask her if I—

JARED   Take off her pants.

ERIC   Take off her pants?

JARED   Yes.

ERIC   Just like that.

JARED   Yes.

ERIC   That's so...

JARED   Dirty.

ERIC   Yeah.

JARED   She likes it dirty.

ERIC   Did I tell you that?

JARED   You did.

> *Beat.*

ERIC   It's weird that I told you that.

JARED   It is weird.

> *Beat.*

ERIC   Why did I tell you that?

JARED   You were having problems with Beth.

ERIC   What kind of problems?

JARED   ...sexual problems.

ERIC   Oh, right. Right.

   I told you that?

> *JARED nods.*

ERIC   Why did I tell you that?

JARED   You thought I could help.

ERIC   Why?

JARED   I edited that documentary about genitalia.

ERIC   I worked on that!

JARED   That's where we met.

ERIC   At the wrap party.

> *Beat.*

That was a long time ago.

JARED   Three years.

ERIC   Didn't I cry on your shoulder?

JARED   You were drunk.

ERIC   I drank a lot back then.

JARED   You still do.

> *Beat*

ERIC   I *almost* assistant directed that film. They said I "wasn't ready."

> *Beat.*

They kept me at grip.

> *Beat.*

JARED   You said you "liked the way I edit."

ERIC   Huh?

JARED   At the screening.

ERIC   You made a cum shot turn into a flower.

> *Beat.*

That was really impressive.

JARED   Not really.

ERIC   No really. It could have looked stupid, but it didn't. You're amazing.

JARED   So are you.

ERIC   I'm a grip.

JARED   You're good at it.

ERIC   Good at what? Moving shit? I move shit. That's what I do for a living.

> *Pause.*

Dirty.

> *Beat.*

JARED   Dirty.

Beat.

ERIC   And if it doesn't work?

JARED   Take a risk.

ERIC   But if it doesn't work?

JARED   Try it.

Beat. Pause.

ERIC   So. How are things with you?

JARED   Just go.

ERIC   I'm serious.

Beat.

JARED   I'm fine.

ERIC   Good. How's the documentary?

JARED   It's fine.

ERIC   Are you working on it?

JARED   No.

ERIC   Why not?

JARED   Because I'm a bad person.

ERIC   No you're not.

JARED   Go.

Beat.

ERIC   Are you sure?

JARED   Yes.

ERIC   We can talk about this if you want.

JARED   Let me know how it goes.

Beat.

ERIC   I love you.

JARED   Right.

ERIC   I do.

Beat.

JARED   I love you too.

ERIC hugs JARED. It's awkwardly intimate. Beat.

Get some gum.

ERIC I only had one.

JARED Get some gum.

ERIC For one beer?

JARED Gum.

Beat.

ERIC Do you have any?

Blackout.

Scene Four – Beth's Work

BETH is preparing to leave. ERIC enters with flowers. He takes out a pack of gum. It is empty.

ERIC *(under his breath)* Shit.

ERIC frantically checks his breath. BETH turns around.

BETH Eric?

ERIC Hey. Surprise.

BETH What are you doing?

ERIC Surprising you.

BETH Why?

ERIC *Why?* I don't know—I thought…. Should I go?

BETH No, just…. Hey. / Sorry. Just… surprised.

ERIC Hey. Is this okay?

BETH Of course. It's more than okay.

BETH's heart melts. She goes to kiss ERIC. He backs away.

What?

ERIC Breath.

BETH Come here.

ERIC No.

BETH Eric!

ERIC Yes?

BETH   Kiss me.

ERIC   No thank you.

> *ERIC backs away. Beat.*

Here.

> *ERIC passes BETH the flowers.*

BETH   Daisies

ERIC   You like daisies?

BETH   I love daisies.

> *She smells them. She's touched. She jumps into ERIC's arms and holds him for a long, important hug. ERIC goes for BETH's pants.*

(backing away) What are you doing?

> *ERIC retreats.*

ERIC   Nothing.

> *Beat.*

BETH   Were you going for my pants?

ERIC   No.

BETH   You were going for my pants.

ERIC   What's wrong with going for your pants?

BETH   I'm at work.

ERIC   You're closed.

BETH   My boss could walk in at *any* moment.

ERIC   More the merrier.

> *ERIC goes for her pants again.*

BETH   Eric stop!

ERIC   What!?

BETH   Are you delirious?

ERIC   Let's have some fun.

BETH   This is not *fun*.

> *He goes for her pants again. She pushes him away.*

ERIC!

ERIC   WHAT?

BETH   This is me, starting to get angry.

ERIC   Angry? I want to give you head and you're angry?

BETH   You think going down on me at work is going to make up for last night?

> *Beat. Yes. Yes he does.*

Why won't you kiss me?

> *Beat. ERIC kisses her. Beat.*

You've been drinking.

ERIC   No, I haven't.

> *Beat.*

BETH   Were you out with Jared?

ERIC   No...

BETH   Are you lying to me?

ERIC   Just, hear me out.

BETH   You're lying to me now?

ERIC   I'm not lying.

BETH   What is wrong / with you?

ERIC   I was out with Jared because I'm concerned about our relationship.

BETH   What does Jared have to do with our relationship?

ERIC   Everything.

BETH   Everything?

ERIC   Not everything, but, he was—he was helping me work through some things.

BETH   What THINGS.

ERIC   About us.

BETH   What, did he tell you to fuck me on an easel?

ERIC   He was helping me put some things into perspective.

> *Beat.*

BETH   Did you tell him about last night?

ERIC   I tell him everything.

BETH Tell ME everything, Eric. Me.

ERIC What's your problem with Jared?

BETH I don't want you talking to him about us.

ERIC We spend a lot of time together.

BETH Are you dependent on him?

ERIC No, we're just very close.

BETH And where do I fit in?

ERIC That's what I'm trying to figure out!

> *Beat.*

BETH With your friend.

ERIC My closest friend.

> *Beat.*

BETH You're working out issues about *our* relationship with your *closest FRIEND.*

ERIC Yes.

BETH And that seems logical to you?

ERIC He understands me.

BETH Does he understand me?

ERIC He's starting to.

> *Beat.*

BETH He doesn't know me. He doesn't know US.

ERIC You can't just come home and expect—

BETH What? To be a priority in your life?

ERIC You *are* a priority.

BETH So treat me better.

ERIC I am! (*beat*) I am.

> *Beat.*

I'm trying.

> *Pause. ERIC kisses BETH. She reciprocates, then stops. Pause.*

BETH I'm tired. I want to go home.

ERIC   I'll make you dinner.

BETH   Why? Because you want to, or because I want you to.

ERIC   Does it matter?

> *Beat.*

BETH   I think I want to be alone tonight.

ERIC   Really?

BETH   I can't, Eric. I can't.... *(beat)* Just... I need to be alone. I need... just tonight. *(beat)* Okay?

ERIC   Where am I supposed to go?

> *She exits.*

Scene Five – Jared's

> *The television is on. It's David Suzuki. ERIC and JARED eat Froot Loops.*

JARED   She's threatened by our relationship.

ERIC   Why?

JARED   She's an insecure woman.

ERIC   But she knows I love her.

JARED   It's not about you.

ERIC   It's not?

JARED   It's her.

ERIC   Her? How?

JARED   You love her?

ERIC   Yes.

JARED   Are you sure?

ERIC   Stop asking me that!

> *Beat.*

JARED   I'm just trying to prove a point—which is that YOU say you love her, but she's still THREATENED by our relationship, which leads me to believe that she's an insecure woman who clearly has some unresolved issues.

ERIC   What kind of issues?

JARED   Well, for starters, she has a hard time with the fact that there are other people in your life that are important to you.

    Beat. ERIC takes a bite of his cereal.

ERIC   These are good.

JARED   They're Froot Loops.

ERIC   Yeah, I like them.

    Beat.

Are there more?

JARED   There's a whole box.

    Beat.

ERIC   Can I have more later?

JARED   Does she know you're here?

ERIC   Who?

JARED   BETH.

ERIC   Yeah, probably.

JARED   Ironic.

ERIC   Why?

JARED   She doesn't want you seeing me, but she makes you stay here.

ERIC   She didn't make me.

JARED   Where else would you go?

    Beat.

ERIC   That is ironic, isn't it.

JARED   It's contradictory behaviour.

ERIC   It is.

    Beat.

ERIC   It's okay that I'm here, right?

JARED   Of course.

ERIC   I can go somewhere else.

JARED   Why?

ERIC   I don't want to be a burden.

JARED   You're not a burden.

> *Beat.*

ERIC   Can you turn that off?

JARED   It's "The Nature of Things."

> *Beat.*

It's David Suzuki.

ERIC   I know who it is.

JARED   We love David Suzuki.

ERIC   I don't love David Suzuki.

JARED   Remember? We watched that episode about the pandas.

ERIC   I love pandas, not David Suzuki.

> *JARED turns off the TV.*

Thank you.

> *Beat.*

Sorry, I just…

> *Beat.*

I don't know what to do.

JARED   What do you think you should do?

ERIC   It's a lot easier with you.

JARED   We're not sleeping together.

ERIC   And if we were, would our relationship become more complicated?

JARED   I think so.

ERIC   Why? Why does it have to be more complicated?

JARED   It's a complicated situation.

ERIC   What is?

JARED   Your relationships.

> *Beat.*

ERIC   I need therapy.

JARED   Good idea.

ERIC   Think so?

JARED   Sure.

>   *Beat.*

ERIC   I don't need therapy.

JARED   Good idea.

>   *Beat. A revelation.*

ERIC   What if you came with me?

JARED   To therapy?

ERIC   To my house.

JARED   When?

ERIC   Tomorrow.

JARED   And do what?

ERIC   Help me.

JARED   Help you what?

ERIC   Make things better.

>   *Beat.*

JARED   How old are you?

ERIC   Twelve.

>   *Beat.*

JARED   What do you want Eric?

ERIC   I want her to NOT be threatened by our relationship. If you came over, she won't feel threatened by our relationship anymore. Maybe she'll understand why we're so close, and then she can feel okay about my relationship to you and to her all at the same time.

>   *Beat.*

JARED   You want me to come over so that you can *fix* your relationships

ERIC   Yes.

JARED   You want me to be your relationship counsellor.

ERIC   EXACTLY!

JARED   Your relationship counsellor.

ERIC   Yes.

JARED   Are you listening to yourself?

ERIC   Yes.

JARED   And that seems like a *normal* request to you.

ERIC   Yes.

JARED   Are you an idiot?

ERIC   Yes.

>   *Beat.*

So?

JARED   No, Eric.

ERIC   Please?

JARED   No.

ERIC   Pretty please?

JARED   How could that possibly be a good idea?

ERIC   It'll make things easier.

JARED   For who? *(Beat. A revelation.)* You're afraid of her.

ERIC   She's scary.

JARED   She's your girlfriend.

ERIC   Aren't you afraid of her?

JARED   I'm not dating her.

ERIC   But you admit she's scary.

JARED   Good. That's great, Eric.

ERIC   It isn't. I know it isn't. But it will be… it'll help if you come.

JARED   How? How will it help?

ERIC   Because it has to.

JARED   I don't think you *really* know what you're doing.

ERIC   I know that Jared, thank you for your delightful insight.

JARED   You wanna go fuck yourself?

ERIC   No. I don't. I really don't. I want to make things better. I'm asking for your help. I *think* it will help. *(beat)*. It could be very helpful.

JARED   It could be very *unhelpful*.

ERIC   Do you have a better idea?

JARED   It's not my responsibility to have a better idea for you.

ERIC   See, that's not helpful.

JARED   So find someone else.

ERIC   There *is* no one else. Okay? I need you. I need us all to just spend some time together. *(beat)* Just fucking help me on this.

> . *Beat.*

JARED   What do you want me to do?

ERIC   Just come over and have dinner.

JARED   What if she doesn't want me over.

ERIC   She will.

JARED   I don't think—

ERIC   She wants to defuse this as much as I do.

JARED   I don't see how—

ERIC   She thinks I'm dependent on you.

JARED   You are.

ERIC   No I'm not.

JARED   You're asking me to come over to your house!

> *Beat.*

ERIC   Okay, I am, but maybe if you come over, it'll help me transfer my dependency over to her—not dependency, but just—I don't know. Loyalty? No, not—

JARED   Love?

> *Beat.*

Remind me: Why are you in this relationship?

> *Beat.*

ERIC   I don't know what else to do.

> *Beat.*

JARED   This makes me really uncomfortable.

ERIC   What can I do to make this more comfortable for you?

JARED   Drugs.

ERIC   Done.

JARED   That's a joke.

> *Beat.*

No, Eric.

ERIC   Yes, Jared.

JARED   That's not a good idea.

ERIC   I think it's a *very* good idea.

JARED   Who are you?

ERIC   I'm Eric. Who are you?

JARED   I'm Jared.

ERIC   Hello Jared, I'm Eric.

JARED   Hello Eric, you're an idiot.

ERIC   No, Jared. No I'm not.

JARED   I'm not doing drugs, with you and your girlfriend who I barely know and who hates me...

ERIC   Yes you will. We all will.

JARED   No we won't.

ERIC   Say you love me.

JARED   No.

ERIC   I love *you*.

JARED   Stop it.

ERIC   Don't you love me?

JARED   No.

ERIC   If you loved me you'd say yes.

JARED   I don't love you.

ERIC   Yes you do.

> *Beat.*

Jared.

> *Beat.*

Jared?

> *Blackout.*

Scene Six – Eric and Beth's – The Dinner

JARED, ERIC and BETH sit around a dinner table. BETH is at the head and the two men sit across from each other. They are eating in silence. Uncomfortable silence. The kind of uncomfortable silence that people work really hard to convince themselves is, in fact, a comfortable silence. A confident silence. An irrelevant silence. But it isn't. It's uncomfortable. It's relevant. It's painful.

JARED   Did we finish the roast?

BETH looks at JARED. He's eaten a lot.

BETH   You were hungry.

JARED   A little.

BETH   There's dessert.

JARED   Great.

Drink. Beat. Drink.

The roast, was…

BETH   Thanks.

JARED   Your recipe?

BETH   My mother's.

Beat.

JARED   Well, tell your mother she's something else.

BETH   She's dead.

JARED   Who.

ERIC   Her mother.

JARED   Oh.

Beat.

I'm sorry.

BETH   It's all right

Beat.

JARED   How did she die?

BETH   I'd rather not talk about it.

JARED   Okay.

Beat.

I'm sorry.

BETH   It was a long time ago.

JARED   I'm surprised Eric never told me.

BETH   Yeah. Me too.

>   *Beat.*

JARED   Well, she lives on in the roast.

>   *Pause.*

BETH   Excuse me.

>   *BETH gets up from the table and leaves the room.*

JARED   What did I say?

>   *Beat.*

ERIC   Her mother died in a fire.

>   *Beat.*

JARED   Are you kidding?

ERIC   She was twelve.

JARED   Why didn't you tell me?

ERIC   I don't know.

JARED   Oh my God.

ERIC   She "lives on in the roast"?

JARED   I'm nervous!

>   *Beat.*

ERIC   She lives on in the roast!?!

JARED   I'm SORRY!

>   *Beat.*

ERIC   I'm going to go check on her.

JARED   Don't leave me alone.

ERIC   I need to see if she's okay.

JARED   *I'M* not okay.

ERIC   I'll be right back!

JARED   Eric!

>   *ERIC gets up from the table. JARED cuts him off.*

JARED   Stay here.

ERIC   Don't be a baby.

JARED   I'm not being a baby.

>   *BETH comes back in. They stop bickering. She sits.*

I am so sorry.

BETH   It's not your fault.

JARED   Still I—

BETH   It's okay.

ERIC   He didn't mean to—

BETH   Can we just... not...?

>   *Beat.*

Thank you.

>   *Beat. JARED and ERIC are frozen.*

So Eric tells me you're editing a film.

JARED   Sorta. Yeah.

ERIC   He's having a tough time right now.

BETH   Why?

ERIC   It's complicated.

JARED   Editing block. Happens sometimes. Stress. Stuff. Stress.

>   *Beat.*

BETH   What's it about?

JARED   Stress probably.

BETH   No, I mean, the film. What's it about?

JARED   Oh. This, uh, shit documentary.

BETH   Not good?

JARED   It's about... shit.

>   *Beat.*

BETH   Shit? Like, poo?

JARED   Poo.

> *Beat. BETH looks at ERIC.*

ERIC   Poo.

> *Beat.*

BETH   Wow.

JARED   It sounds…

BETH   Great. It sounds great.

JARED   It sounds stupid.

BETH   No it / doesn't.

JARED   I know it sounds stupid

BETH   You don't have to—

JARED   I need the money.

BETH   There's nothing wrong with that.

JARED   It's…. No… there's nothing wrong…

> *Beat.*

How was your trip?

BETH   It was fantastic. Thank you. For asking.

> *Beat.*

JARED   Eric told me you went to see some art.

BETH   I did.

JARED   See anything good?

BETH   I did.

JARED   Good. Good for you.

> *Beat.*

I hear the men in Spain are really attractive.

BETH   I wouldn't know.

JARED   Didn't look?

BETH   I've never been to Spain.

JARED   I'm sorry?

BETH   I was in Italy.

> *Beat.*

Did you tell him I was in *Spain*?

ERIC   No.

JARED   Yes you did.

ERIC   I meant Italy.

JARED   No, you were pretty sure—

ERIC   Fuck off Jared.

BETH   You thought I was in *Spain?*

ERIC   I know you were in Italy.

BETH   What was I doing in Italy?

ERIC   Art classes.

BETH   Art classes? What kind of *art* classes.

> *Beat.*

You were there when I applied. We talked about why it was important for me to go.

ERIC   I know you took an art class.

BETH   RENAISSANCE ART.

ERIC   Renaissance Art.

BETH   In ITALY

ERIC   There are a lot of attractive men in Spain AND Italy.

BETH   There's no Spain. Okay? No Spain. Just Italy, and yes, the men are gorgeous.

ERIC   I know they are.

BETH   How do you know?

ERIC   Jared's been.

BETH   You've been to Italy?

JARED   Spain.

BETH   I wasn't *in* Spain.

> *Beat.*

You thought I was in *SPAIN?*

ERIC   I made a mistake.

BETH   SPAIN?

ERIC   They're both Spanish countries.

BETH   NO THEY AREN'T.

ERIC   They sound Spanish.

BETH   They're entirely different languages.

JARED   There are similarities.

BETH   LIKE WHAT?

JARED   The colouring of the people, some of the architecture, the cultural pride…. It's not uncommon for Westerners to confuse the two.

BETH   Did you tell Eric to fuck me at my art store?

JARED   No.

BETH   Are you lying?

ERIC   Shut up, Jared.

JARED   I told him to eat you out.

ERIC   SHUT UP, Jared.

BETH   This! This is the person helping you put things into PERSPECTIVE.

JARED   Have you always been such a bitch?

ERIC   What—No. No no no no no no no.

BETH   You think I'm a bitch?

ERIC   No. He doesn't.

BETH   Am I a bitch?

ERIC   No. Jared apologize. Tell her she's not a bitch. You're not a bitch.

BETH   *(to JARED)* Is that what you think?

ERIC   JARED! You're not a bitch.

BETH   You don't even know me.

JARED   I know what I hear.

BETH   What did you tell him?

ERIC   I never said you were a bitch.

JARED   You're controlling.

ERIC   I didn't say that.

JARED   Yes you did.

ERIC   Jared, please, don't do this.

JARED   Someone needs to tell her.

BETH   Tell her what?

>   *Beat.*

JARED   Eric thinks you're scary. So do I.

>   *Beat.*

BETH   Is that true? *(beat)* Eric?

>   *Beat.*

You're not the only one who's scared.

>   *Beat.*

I'm scared too.

You're scary too.

>   *Beat.*

JARED   Why can't Eric come to me for advice?

BETH   It's about *our* relationship. Ours. Not yours.

JARED   It affects me too.

BETH   How? How does it affect you?

JARED   Do I threaten you?

BETH   *(point to Eric)* No. *He* threatens me. *You* annoy the *fuck* out of me.

ERIC   Beth, please can we / calm down.

BETH   Am I making you uncomfortable, Eric?

JARED   You're making us *all* uncomfortable.

BETH   You edit movies about shit!

JARED   You work in an art *STORE*. You sell PENCIL crayons. And you? What do you do? You don't do shit. All you do is bitch and complain about HER. Every fucking day, it's all I hear. For six months all I hear about is you, and then you come back and y'know what, I think maybe he's justified in—

ERIC   Jared!

>   *Beat.*

JARED   Someone needs to tell her this.

ERIC   It's time for you to leave.

JARED   You're afraid of her.

ERIC   That's not—

JARED   What kind of person dates someone he's afraid of?

ERIC   I DO.

JARED   That's right! And who has to deal with it?

ERIC   You need to leave.

JARED .   Oh, what, is it not convenient to have me here anymore?

ERIC   GET OUT.

JARED   Am I not acting the way you want me to?

ERIC   No, you're not, you're acting like a fucking psycho!

JARED   Fuck you. Fuck you both.

> *Beat.*

> *(to ERIC)* How can you possibly live like this?

> *Beat.*

BETH   I think you go now.

JARED   You started this.

BETH   Yeah, I started it. *(beat)* I started it. I'm the one. It was me. ME! I'm the BITCH and you're the fags. I'm the bitch. It's me. I'm the bitch, guys. HEY LOOK OVER HERE. IT'S ME. BITCH GIRL. I'M HERE TO BITCH YOU ALL THE WAY TO BITCH HELL. AND IT'S A BEAUTIFUL HELL. IT'S THE MOST MAGNIFICENT HELL YOU'VE EVER LAID EYES ON. AND BEING THERE TOGETHER WILL MAKE IT BEAUTIFUL. *(pause)* What was it we took again?

ERIC   Ecstasy.

BETH   I think I feel it.

JARED   I'm high.

ERIC   Me too.

BETH   Wow. *(beat)* Holy Shit.

ERIC   Are you okay?

BETH   I'm *so* okay.

> *Beat.*

> *BETH gets up and stands on her chair. (Could be a couch, in which case, substitute the word "chair" for "couch.")*

Is it okay if I do this?

ERIC   Absolutely.

BETH   I just feel like doing this. Do you guys wanna do this?

JARED   ·Stand… on the…?

BETH   It's really nice up here.

> *Beat.*

ERIC   Okay. *(ERIC gets on the chair.)* Get on your chair.

JARED   I'm gonna go.

ERIC   Why?

JARED   I thought you wanted me to.

ERIC   I do, but—get on the chair first.

JARED   Why?

ERIC   Because it's *nice.*

> *JARED gets on the chair.*

BETH   Is there wind?

JARED   No.

ERIC   Yes.

> *ERIC begins to blow on BETH.*

BETH   Oh! Yes. Yes, keep doing that.

ERIC   Blow on her.

JARED   I'm not blowing on her.

BETH   Blow on me, Jared. Blow on me. *(beat)* Please.

> *JARED blows on BETH. The two men stand blowing on her for a brief period. It is absurd, sexual and uncomfortable.*

JARED   Maybe someone should put some music on?

BETH   Oh let me!

JARED   I can do it.

BETH   Please let me do it. Please. It'll be so much fun.

Before JARED has a chance to protest, BETH hops off her chair and makes her way out of the room. The two men stand there in silence.

(off) There's so much to choose from!

The men continue standing. Looking at each other. Getting higher and higher with each passing second.

(off) Any preferences!?

Getting higher. ERIC comes onto the middle chair. Higher. JARED joins him. They stand, practically nose to nose. They can feel each other's breath.

ERIC kisses JARED. JARED returns the kiss and ERIC pushes JARED away.

(off) Oh! This is good!

Music blares. It is blatant Italian dance music. It is loud, and it breaks the men up. ERIC backs away. BETH comes dancing on. The two men are standing in relative stillness. ERIC makes a beeline to BETH and kisses her passionately.

The two start to dance together. JARED watches. He gets off his chair. He is high and confused. He continues to watch them. BETH takes off ERIC's shirt. JARED still watches. BETH kisses ERIC's body. ERIC lets her—enjoying every minute of it.

JARED, overwhelmed, leaves.

BETH and ERIC continue to dance and devour each other, while the lights slowly fade to black.

Scene Seven

ERIC in a spotlight.

ERIC   Hey, it's Eric.

Beat.

This is my cell. This is the message. This is the beep.

Beep. Spot on JARED

JARED   Hey. It's Jared. *(beat)* Hey. Just calling to… yeah. How are you? Haven't heard from you in a couple weeks. Thought you may want to go for a drink, or… a baseball game or… *(beat)* Shit. *(beat)* Not SHIT, but uhhh. So. Hope you're well. I'm good. I lost the contract on the film, which sucks, but y'know… *(beat)* Say hi to… *(beat)* `Kay. Bye. *(beat)* Bye. *(beat)* Call me back. *(beat)* Bye. *(beat)* Call me back.

JARED hangs up.

MACHINE   Message deleted.

ERIC   *(voice-over)* Hey, it's Eric. This is my cell. This is the message. This is the beep.

Beep. Spot on BETH.

BETH   Hi. It's late. Just got home. Where are you?

MACHINE   Message deleted.

JARED   Hey, it's me again—

MACHINE   Message deleted.

BETH   Hey. You were gone before I woke up, so, hope the job hunt is going well.

MACHINE   Message deleted.

JARED   Hey. I called like a couple days ago and—

MACHINE   Message deleted.

BETH   Was hoping we'd get the chance to—

MACHINE   Message deleted.

JARED   So, it's Jared. Just thought I'd—

> *The scene begins to loop itself, starting with BETH's: "Hi, it's late." The same scene also begins to loop in voice over, picking up in pace, until there is a frenzied chaos onstage that comes to a blistering halt with:*

MACHINE   Message deleted. Message deleted. Message deleted. Message deeeeeelllllleeeeeetttttteeeeeed.

Scene Eight – Eric And Beth's

> *Lights up on BETH. She paints. Music plays (song from beginning of the play). JARED enters.*

JARED   Where is he?

BETH   *(startled)* Jesus!

JARED   Where is he?

BETH   What are you doing?

JARED   Eric!

BETH   How did you get in?

JARED   I have a key. ERIC!?

BETH   You have a key?

JARED   Eric gave me a key. ERIC!

BETH   He's not here.

JARED   Where is he?

BETH   He's not here. Please leave.

JARED   I heard music.

BETH   Did you think it was a party?

JARED   I thought it was Eric, listening to music.

BETH   Why not me?

JARED   You're listening to the CD I made him.

BETH   You made him a CD?

JARED   A couple months ago.

> *Beat. BETH turns off the CD.*

BETH   It's a good CD.

JARED   Thank you.

> *Beat.*

BETH   Would you please go?

JARED   Where's Eric?

BETH   Not home. I'll tell him you were here.

JARED   Do you know when he'll be home?

BETH   I don't.

> *Beat.*

JARED   Where is he?

BETH   I don't know.

JARED   You'll tell him I was here.

BETH   When I see him.

JARED   When will that be?

BETH   I don't know, Jared.

BETH nods her head. Beat.

JARED   Will you just... will you tell him I was here? *(beat)* Please?

BETH   Yes! Yes!

JARED   Okay. I'm going. Okay? I'm going. I'm sorry, I didn't mean to... I'm going.

    JARED inches away.

BETH   May I have your key?

JARED   Why?

BETH   It's important that Eric and I speak together before we give people keys to our home.

JARED   You weren't here when he gave it to me.

BETH   I'm here now.

JARED   He didn't *speak* to you, because you weren't here.

BETH   I realize that.

JARED   He doesn't just *give keys away.*

BETH   I know.

JARED   No, you don't. He gave *me* a key. ME. I'm not just *anybody.*

    Beat.

    JARED goes to exit.

BETH   Jared.

    Beat.

The key.

    JARED digs into his pocket for the key. He brings it to BETH.

Thank you.

    Beat. JARED goes to exit. JARED sees the painting BETH has been working on. He stops.

    JARED walks up to the painting.

JARED   This yours?

BETH   Yes.

    JARED looks at it.

JARED   It's...

BETH   It's fine.

JARED   No, it's really… it's…

> *Pause.*

Look, I…

> *Beat.*

BETH   You don't have to—

JARED   No, I… just…

> *Pause. JARED goes to exit. He stops and takes in the painting again.*

Do you mind if I just look at this for a sec?

> *Beat.*

Sorry, I'm being…

BETH   Go ahead.

> *JARED looks at the painting. BETH watches him watching the painting.*

JARED   Do you have any more?

BETH   I do.

> *Beat.*

JARED   May I see them?

BETH   Now?

JARED   No! Not—I mean, yes, of course, but that's not what I meant.

> *Beat.*

But if you felt like showing them now…

> *BETH does not move.*

Sorry, is this…?

BETH   No. Sure. I'll show you.

JARED   You don't have to if you don't want to.

BETH   I want to.

> *BETH exits. JARED returns to the painting. He once again gets lost in it.*
>
> *She has another painting and a few drawings. She hangs them up or spreads them on the floor. She stands away from them, freeing the*

> *area for JARED to see. JARED moves to the artwork and beings to look through them.*

JARED   This one's really good.

> *Beat.*

BETH   That's Eric's favourite.

> *Beat.*

JARED   Did you do these in Italy?

BETH   A couple. I left most of my canvases in Florence.

JARED   Don't you want them?

BETH   I was hoping to sell a few.

JARED   Is that hard?

BETH   I could get lucky.

JARED   Leaving them there, I mean. Is it hard having to part with them?

> *Beat.*

BETH   Yeah. It is. It was. It's getting easier.

> *Beat.*

JARED   I just lost my job.

BETH   I know.

JARED   How?

BETH   On your message.

JARED   You listened to my messages?

BETH   It's *my* answering machine.

JARED   Did you delete them?

BETH   No.

JARED   Did Eric?

BETH   I don't know.

JARED   Did he listen to them?

BETH   Yes.

JARED   Are you sure?

BETH   Positive.

    Beat.

JARED   Did you tell him not to return my calls?

BETH   No.

JARED   Are you lying?

    Beat.

BETH   You should probably go.

JARED   Are you lying to me?

    Beat. BETH glares at JARED.

Just tell me if you're lying to me.

BETH   What is wrong with you?

JARED   I don't like it when people lie to me.

BETH   I don't like it when people accuse me of lying.

JARED   I'm not accusing you, I'm—

    Beat.

I haven't talked to him in two weeks.

BETH   Neither have I.

JARED   What do you mean?

BETH   I barely see him.

JARED   Why?

BETH   I don't know why. I stopped asking.

    Beat.

He says he's looking for a job.

    Beat.

I assumed he's been spending time with you.

JARED   I don't understand.

BETH   There's not much to understand.

JARED   He's avoiding you?

    Pause.

BETH   Can you please go now.

    Beat.

Please?

Beat.

Please...

Pause.

JARED   You're not a bitch.

Beat.

BETH   I know.

Beat.

JARED   I shouldn't have said that.

BETH   I know.

Beat.

JARED   And... I apologize.

Beat.

BETH   Thank you

Beat.

I appreciate... your... apology.

Beat.

JARED   Good. I mean.... Good. I'm glad—that makes me.... I'm...

Pause.

BETH   Do you want to see some photos from Florence?

JARED   Okay.

BETH runs out of the room. JARED sits again. He goes back to the drawings. He spots one. It's of ERIC. He's naked. He picks it up and stares. We see the drawing projected. It's a charcoal of ERIC's naked body. BETH returns.

BETH   I found a few rolls...

BETH sees what he's looking at. She sits down next to JARED. They stare at the drawing.

I used to draw him all the time.

JARED   He has a nice body.

BETH   He does.

> *Beat. JARED continues to stare at the drawing.*

Are you...?

> *Beat.*

JARED   No.

> *Beat.*

BETH   So you never...?

> *Beat.*

JARED   No.

> *Pause.*

BETH   Do you wanna see...?

JARED   Sure.

> *Beat. BETH takes out some of the pictures. They are in picture books. Before she opens:*

BETH   The birthplace of the Renaissance.

JARED   Is that important?

BETH   Is that a joke?

JARED   Yes.

> *Beat. BETH opens the book.*

Is that what you studied?

BETH   It was my primary. I'm more interested in abstracts.

JARED   Learning your trade.

BETH   Exactly.

> *Beat.*

Here, look. (*She shows a photo.*) That's a wide angle of the Piazza de la Signora. It's the main square in Florence.

JARED   It's brilliant.

> *Beat.*

> *She takes another photo.*

BETH   You know what this is.

JARED   David.

BETH Y'know how when you've been told that something is beautiful, and then you see it, and it's just as beautiful...?

JARED The Alhambra Palace.

BETH Sorry?

JARED It's a castle... in Spain.

BETH You've actually been?

JARED One year my parents decided to take me on their "vacation" instead of kennelling me with the grandparents.

BETH Have you been back?

> *JARED shakes his head "no."*

It's different... when you're older.

JARED What is?

BETH Just... going away. It's... different.

> *Beat.*
>
> *Another photo.*

This is "Perseus."

JARED Who's the artist?

BETH Cellini. It's really famous.

JARED Is that...?

BETH Medusa.

JARED Yeah! Why is he holding her head?

BETH He chopped it off.

JARED Why?

BETH I don't know. Maybe she scorned him.

JARED Maybe he scorned her. *(beat)* Doesn't matter.

BETH Why doesn't it matter?

JARED He won.

> *Beat.*

BETH This isn't boring for you is it?

JARED No, It's an amazing picture.

BETH Photography's not really my...

JARED kisses BETH. She allows him, at first, but then gently pushes him away. Pause.

JARED   I...

> *Beat. Pause.*

I don't know why I did that.

BETH   Okay. *(beat)* Was it my fault?

JARED   I don't think so. *(beat)* Sorry.

BETH   Me too.

> *Beat.*

Maybe you should / go.

JARED   Yeah.

BETH   It's fine. Just... I think... I think you / should go.

JARED   I'm gonna go.

BETH   Okay.

> *Beat. JARED goes to exit.*

JARED   I didn't mean to do that.

BETH   Can you just... sorry... can you... go?

> *Beat.*

JARED   I'll go.

> *JARED exits.*

BETH   Fuck.

> *Lights go black.*

Scene Nine – Jared's

> *ERIC sits on JARED's bed. JARED enters. Pause.*

JARED   What are you doing here?

ERIC   You have a big stain on your wall.

JARED   Did you break into my house?

ERIC   Your place smells.

JARED   Why are you here?

ERIC   You gave me a key.

JARED   Why? Why did we do that?

> *Beat.*

What do you want?

ERIC   What do *you* want?

> *Beat.*

Why do you keep calling?

JARED   Because I'm your friend.

ERIC   It's just—you keep calling, and it's getting annoying.

JARED   Oh is it?

ERIC   Yeah, it is, so you can stop.

JARED   Yeah, fine.

ERIC   Thanks.

JARED   You're welcome, asshole.

ERIC   You want your key back?

JARED   Yeah, I want my key back.

ERIC   Come and get it.

JARED   Give it to me.

ERIC   It's right here.

JARED   Give me the fucking key.

ERIC   Why don't you come get it?

JARED   Fine.

> *JARED moves to get the key back from ERIC. ERIC doesn't give it. They begin to wrestle. It's violent and homoerotic. It gets more violent. They continue to wrestle. JARED manages to pin ERIC to the bed. He stops. He looks down at ERIC. Pause.*

ERIC   Do you wanna fuck me?

> *Beat.*

Do you?

JARED   No.

> *ERIC pushes JARED off him.*
>
> *Beat.*

ERIC   You kissed me.

JARED   You kissed *me.*

ERIC   I thought that's what you wanted.

JARED   To fuck you?

ERIC   I don't know!

>*Beat.*

I don't know what you want from me.

JARED   A friend, Eric.

ERIC   I can't be your friend.

JARED   Why not?

ERIC   Because maybe you were right. I can't have two pussies.

>*Beat.*

JARED   Are you afraid of me?

ERIC   Yes.

JARED   Why?

>*Beat.*

Tell me why.

ERIC   You know why.

JARED   Tell me.

ERIC   Us. Our relationship. Everything.

>*Beat.*

JARED   I make you insecure.

ERIC   Yes, exactly.

JARED   And your world revolves around your insecurities.

ERIC   It does.

JARED   And you don't see that as being a problem? This world you've created for yourself… does it seem in any way problematic?

ERIC   I didn't create—

JARED   Have you ever seen Cellini's "Perseus"?

ERIC   What's that?

JARED   It's in Florence.

ERIC   So?

JARED   It's pretty amazing.

ERIC   And...?

JARED   It's this bronze soldier who has Medusa in his hands, and—

ERIC   How does this in ANY WAY pertain to what we're talking about?

JARED   Y'know what, it doesn't.

ERIC   That's really, *really* interesting JARED.

JARED   It's a fuck load more interesting than listening to you bitch and moan about your bullshit insecurities. We all have insecurities Eric, and y'know what, they're boring as shit. Y'know what IS interesting though? Cellini's "Perseus." That's fucking interesting.

ERIC   Then why don't you just go to Florence and take a picture.

JARED   Beth already did.

ERIC   Did what?

JARED   She took a picture, and she showed me, and it's beautiful.

ERIC   When did you see Beth?

JARED   Earlier today.

ERIC   Were you at my house?

JARED   I was looking for you.

> *Beat.*

ERIC   I don't want you at my house when I'm not there.

JARED   It's her house too.

ERIC   I don't want you there.

JARED   Are you afraid that she'll leave you for me?

ERIC   Yes, Jared. I'm afraid she'll leave me for you.

JARED   You don't think that could happen?

ERIC   No, I don't—

JARED   So then what are you afraid of?

ERIC   I'm not afraid of anything.

JARED   So then what's your problem with me being at your house when you're not there?

ERIC   My problem is that I don't like you, and I don't want people that I don't like in my home, ever. I don't care if I'm there or not, I don't want you there, because I DON'T LIKE YOU. Is that understood?

>   *Beat.*

JARED   Fine.

>   *Beat. ERIC lightly smacks JARED.*

ERIC   Stay out of my home.

JARED   Fine. Maybe it's for the best.

ERIC   What does that mean?

JARED   It means maybe you should put a little more focus into your relationship.

ERIC   Thanks for the tip.

JARED   You're welcome.

ERIC   Fat piece of shit.

>   *ERIC exits. Beat.*

>   *Blackout.*

Scene Ten – Eric And Beth's

>   *ERIC walks in. BETH is dialing the phone. She puts the phone down.*

BETH   Hey.

ERIC   Hey.

>   *ERIC comes up to BETH and starts to kiss her. BETH pulls away gently.*

BETH   Hi?

ERIC   Hi.

>   *ERIC takes off his shirt and starts to kiss BETH again. BETH kisses him back. They start to get into it. ERIC starts to take off BETH's pants.*

BETH   Wait.

ERIC   What?

BETH Just wait a second.

ERIC Why?

BETH Because Eric!

> *Beat. ERIC sits back, his shirt still off. BETH pulls up her pants.*

ERIC What are you doing?

BETH I don't want to.

ERIC Why not?

BETH This is the first time I've seen you in, what? Three days?

ERIC I saw you this morning.

BETH We passed each other on the way to the washroom.

> *Beat.*

Do you love me?

ERIC What?

> *Beat.*

Is that a joke?

> *Beat.*

Yes, I love you.

BETH Why?

ERIC Because I do.

BETH What do you love about me?

> *Beat.*

ERIC What are you doing?

BETH Attempting communication.

ERIC Things have been going well.

BETH Well? You think things have been going *well*?

ERIC We've been busy.

BETH We've found time to fuck.

ERIC So?

BETH All we do is fuck.

ERIC You say that like it's a bad thing.

BETH You're my *partner,* Eric, not my fuck-buddy.

ERIC I know—

BETH You have to be PRESENT to be my partner.

ERIC What?

BETH You're avoiding me.

ERIC Beth—

BETH Can you not call me that?

ERIC Call you what?

BETH Beth. My name. Shortened like that. My name is Elizabeth.

ERIC I've always called you Beth.

BETH Do you not have the *energy* to call me by my full name?

ERIC It's a nickname. A pet name.

BETH I'm not a nick, or a pet. I'm your girlfriend. Use my girlfriend name.

> *Pause.*

Say something.

> *Beat.*

ERIC I don't know what to say?

BETH Tell me why you love me.

ERIC You know why I love you.

BETH No, Eric. I don't.

ERIC Why do you love me?

> *Beat.*

It's a difficult question.

BETH Should it be?

> *Beat.*

ERIC You went away for a really long time.

BETH We agreed—

ERIC And then you come home, and you just… you start making all these…

BETH What? All these what?

ERIC I don't know! I don't—

BETH Eric, I just want you to be good to me.

> *Beat.*

ERIC It was hard when you left.

BETH It was hard for me too.

ERIC Then why did you go?

BETH You know why.

ERIC No. I thought I did. But then when you left, it was as if…. It was a long time for us to be apart.

BETH Would you rather I'd not gone at all?

ERIC I think so.

> *Beat.*

BETH We agreed.

ERIC I know, but still…

> *Beat.*

It was scary.

BETH I know.

We agreed that we can't *not* do things because we're afraid.

ERIC That didn't make it any easier.

BETH It's not supposed to be easy.

ERIC Why?

BETH Because life, is, hard. Have you not figured that out yet, Eric?

> *Beat.*

It was hard for me too. I was in a strange country—nobody spoke English. I had to learn Italian. I was away from you.

> *Beat.*

You know it was hard. How many times did I call you in tears? How many emails did I send…?

ERIC Sometimes three a day.

BETH Yah!

> *Beat.*

But I needed to go to Italy. I wasn't doing anything. I cooked and I fucked you. That was my life. I *needed* to go to Italy.

ERIC   What about what I need?

BETH   I don't know what you need. I never know what you need. Do you know what you need?

> *Beat. Pause.*

ERIC   I need for Jared to not be here when I'm not here?

BETH   What?

ERIC   Jared. He was here. Why?

BETH   How do you know that?

ERIC   He told me.

> *Beat.*

BETH   He was here looking for you.

ERIC   And then he, what? He stayed? He stayed and you showed him pictures?

BETH   Yes.

ERIC   Why.

BETH   Because I felt like.

ERIC   Since when do you feel like spending time with Jared?

BETH   I thought that's what you wanted.

> *Beat.*

ERIC   I don't trust him.

BETH   Do you trust me?

ERIC   Did something happen?

BETH   Do you trust me?

ERIC   Yes, I trust you, it's *him* I don't trust.

> *Beat.*

What happened?

BETH   Nothing happened.

> *Beat.*

ERIC   I don't believe you.

BETH   NOTHING HAPPENED.

> *Beat.*

ERIC   Are you sure?

BETH   POSITIVE.

> *Beat.*

ERIC   We just...

> *Beat.*

I'm sorry, we... we fought. We had a big fight.

> *Beat.*

I think it's over. Me and Jared.

> *Pause.*

Can I see your photos from Florence?

BETH   Right now?

ERIC   Sure.

BETH   It's late.

ERIC   I don't mind.

> *Beat.*

BETH   Okay.

> *Beat. BETH exits for the photos. ERIC sits. Void. She comes back on with a few rolls. She sits on the couch. ERIC makes a move to join her. He sits down next to her. She starts to flip through them.*

ERIC   You're going too fast.

BETH   Sorry.

ERIC   It's okay.

> *ERIC takes the photos himself and flips through them, (as fast or faster than BETH). He finds what he's looking for. Beat.*

Is that "Perseus"?

BETH   Yes. How'd you know that?

ERIC   Jared told me about it.

BETH   Really?

ERIC   Yeah. What's in his hands?

BETH   Medusa.

ERIC   What's that?

BETH   The legend was that when they looked at her, men turned to stone, so Perseus chopped off her head.

> *ERIC examines the photo.*

ERIC   Why is he naked?

BETH   He was probably trying to fuck her.

ERIC   But he killed her instead?

BETH   Maybe he killed her, then fucked her torso.

> *Beat.*

ERIC   Right...

> *They continue to look at the photos for a few seconds.*

I should get to bed.

BETH   Good idea.

> *BETH makes a move to leave.*

ERIC   I love you.

> *Beat.*

BETH   I love you too.

> *Beat. BETH Exits.*

Scene Eleven – Eric And Beth's

ERIC   And when I got back the next day, she was gone.

JARED   Just like that.

ERIC   Just like that. Packed her bags, and left.

> *Beat.*

JARED   Where did she go?

ERIC   I don't know. Her mother's?

JARED   Her mother's dead.

ERIC   Right. *(beat)* Then I don't know.

> *Pause.*

JARED   So that's it?

ERIC   What's it?

JARED   It's over?

ERIC   I don't know. Does this mean it's over?

> *Beat.*

What do you think?

JARED   I don't know.

> *Beat.*

ERIC   Do you have any advice at all?

JARED   Not really.

ERIC   Not really?

JARED   Nope.

> *Beat.*

ERIC   Should I go after her?

JARED   I don't know.

ERIC   Do you think it would help?

JARED   I don't know.

> *Beat.*

ERIC   I'm a total mess.

JARED   It's a tough situation. *(pause)* Listen, I hate to do this… *(beat)* I have to go.

ERIC   Why?

JARED   I've got to work.

ERIC   On what?

JARED   I got the shit thing back.

ERIC   How?

JARED   They sorta begged me. Offered me more money.

ERIC   Wow. *(beat)* That's great. That's amazing.

> *Beat.*

So, when are you free?

JARED   I'm pretty busy with this thing.

Beat.

ERIC Okay. Can I call you later?

JARED Well… believe it or not, I've got a date.

ERIC You do?

JARED Neat, huh?

ERIC With whom?

JARED A dancer.

ERIC Where did you meet?

JARED At an art opening.

ERIC Since when do you go to art openings?

JARED I know… weird.

Beat.

ERIC What's her name?

JARED Tanya.

ERIC You're dating a girl named Tanya?

JARED She has an incredible torso.

ERIC laughs. It goes on too long.

ERIC So, I guess you go.

JARED Okay.

Beat.

ERIC Give me a call when you're free.

JARED I will.

Pause.

ERIC Can I have a hug?

JARED Sure.

JARED hugs ERIC. A very different hug. A very "male" hug. Beat.

ERIC I love you.

Beat.

JARED I love you too.

Beat.

ERIC   Okay. Bye.

JARED   Bye.

> *Beat.*

ERIC   Bye.

JARED   Bye.

> *Pause.*

Bye.

> *JARED exits.*

ERIC   Bye.

> *Blackout.*
>
> *End of Play.*

photo by Michael Lee

Dave Carley is a Toronto-based playwright who writes for theatre, radio and television. His stage plays have had over three hundred productions across Canada, the US, and in a dozen countries around the world. They include *Conservatives in Love, The Edible Woman, Walking on Water* and *Writing With Our Feet,* which was nominated for a Governor-General's Literary Award. Dave is currently playwright-in-residence at the Shaw Festival, where he is working on a drama about Danish playwright and war hero Kaj Munk. In July 2008, Dave will make his directing debut at the Toronto Fringe Festival, with his play *Taking Liberties.* Dave's website is www.davecarley.com.